The Way of a Pilgrim

The Way of a Pilgrim

Translated by

Nina A. Toumanova

Foreword by

Norris J. Chumley, PhD

ixia PRESS

Mineola, New York

Bibliographical Note

This Ixia Press edition, first published in 2019, is an unabridged republication of the work as it appeared in *A Treasury of Russian Spirituality*, edited by G. P. Fedetov and printed by Sheed and Ward, London, 1950. A new foreword by Norris J. Chumley, PhD has been specially prepared for this volume.

International Standard Book Number

ISBN-13: 978-0-486-82368-3
ISBN-10: 0-486-82368-7

Ixia Press
An imprint of Dover Publications, Inc.

Manufactured in the United States by LSC Communications
82368701 2019
www.doverpublications.com/ixiapress

FOREWORD

Hello and welcome, Pilgrim.

Yes, that is who we are: spiritual travelers, pilgrims on voyages to new experiences and life changes—just like the anonymous author of *The Way of a Pilgrim.*

I guess that you must be looking for God through prayer and want to learn about the best method, as did our mystical seeker. You and I and our pilgrim friend have much in common. We are aspirants of the ultimate truth, determined to find and know God. I am not aware of what circumstances you're in or who sent you, yet I know you very well. This is because I, too, am a pilgrim on the journey of a lifetime to the ultimate encounter with the Creator, through prayer—specifically, "the Jesus Prayer."

"Lord Jesus Christ, son of God, have mercy on me, a sinner." These twelve words contain the essence of a Christian life. This simple prayer acknowledges Jesus as the Christ, the son of God, here with us, divine and human at the same time. It offers us repentance of our mistakes and sins and a petition for God's mercy and forgiveness. You may have heard of the Jesus Prayer, sometimes called "the Prayer of the Heart." However, since I converted to Greek Orthodox Christianity over a decade ago, I regularly encounter many people—"religious," "spiritual," or not—who do not know this all-powerful prayer, much less use it in their daily lives.

Like our companion pilgrim, you also may have had some difficulties. Most everyone has. It may very well be that you've had some truly terrifying or life-threatening circumstances. It may be that right now you are suffering or are in trouble and are looking for relief, a way out. You are not alone. The pilgrim and I are with you. In essence, we are all pilgrims thirsting for God. I have had many hardships, and very much like the pilgrim, I looked for God through prayer, and God has helped and rescued me many times and continues to guide and love me.

As you read the pilgrim's adventures and the sojourn stops along the way, you'll encounter many vicissitudes: he admits he was a heavy drinker and out-of-control; got demoted from his position in the army; was robbed by thieves; was falsely accused and arrested for sexual abuse of a young girl; was whipped and beaten; lost the use of his legs and an arm from a fight with his brother. It's truly a set of harrowing trials for the poor soul. I hope your life isn't as bad. Yet through it all, the Jesus Prayer brought the pilgrim directly to God, granting him safety and rescue. Jesus and his teachings through the Gospels, along with continual prayer, brought him freedom and relief. At one point, he mentions that such salvation made him feel like he'd been made czar, the Russian equivalent of an emperor or king.

Yet, the pilgrim is so humble that he wrote this travelogue and soul-guide anonymously, clearly as a gift for us. We don't know much of anything about him. Yet he drops clues like bread crumbs on a trail: writing about feeling like a czar; saying he was a soldier in the Russian army; being "born in a village in the province of Orel." Other mentions of specific historical points place him in Russia in the nineteenth century.

It's also profoundly clear that the pilgrim was highly determined. Setting out on his pilgrimage, armed with only a treasured Bible and a string of prayer beads, he stopped at nothing to discover the true and correct method of prayer, to experience God firsthand. He strove to follow a teaching of Saint Paul's: "to pray without ceasing." He fervently prayed to have the Jesus Prayer start on his lips and travel to his mind and heart. He did not give up trying until he was in direct communication with God. He wrote, "When I called upon the name of Jesus, I would be overwhelmed with bliss, and the meaning of 'the kingdom of heaven is within you' emanates from Christ himself"—and into the entire being of the pilgrim. I want to experience that too. Don't you?

The pilgrim also shares some words of caution: the importance of finding and following a *starets* (a spiritual elder); to go to church; to start slowly; to not get instantly overzealous and try to pray unceasingly right at the beginning. There is plenty of time—a lifetime.

As I write this foreword, I am sitting on a balcony, overlooking the Aegean Sea, at the Holy and Great Monastery of Vatopedi on the Mount Athos peninsula in Greece, home for over one thousand years to about twenty ancient living monasteries and little else. I am silently praying the Jesus Prayer and asking God to help you begin your own pilgrimage of love and direct connection with God. I also have asked for words of counsel and consolation from the monks and the head of the monastery, Elder Ephraim. The abbot simply says, with an easy, loving smile but also in all seriousness, "Tell them to start by praying the Jesus Prayer only when they have some free time."

Every monk I've spoken with here on the holy mountain has told me that their spiritual lives began by reading *The Way of a Pilgrim*. It is truly a treasured classic. This book is not only a beautiful spiritual starting point, but it also has been a divine door to ultimate peace, freedom, and salvation for millions of people over many years.

But please don't think that you need to become a cloistered monk to use it. Although I love church and heartily recommend it, you don't have to go anywhere at all to try it. The Jesus Prayer is for everyone, everywhere, in whatever place or circumstance or degree of pain or suffering, right here, right now. I would add that if it is too much for you to begin reciting the prayer over and over, you might consider just closing your eyes for a moment, taking three slow deep breaths, and saying the holy name of Jesus along with your breathing. And if that is too much, try saying his name or the prayer just once. Or quietly, in your inner heart, humbly ask God for help. Then dive in and start reading *The Way of a Pilgrim*, letting God direct your steps on your journey. Above all, with the Jesus Prayer and these loving stories, you are already on your way. And for that, I thank God unceasingly.

Know that the monks and I pray for you, as did the pilgrim, who gave us his very best by writing about his prayerful journey. And if you feel like it and have some free time, I ask you to pray the Jesus Prayer for me, too, because we're all in need of God's help and guidance as fellow pilgrims on the way.

With love,
Norris J. Chumley, PhD

"THE PILGRIM" ON MENTAL PRAYER

The Candid Narrations of a Pilgrim to His Spiritual Father was first printed in Kazan' in 1884. It soon became a rare book, considered to be almost esoteric and held in high esteem by all searchers into the ways of Orthodox mysticism. Only recently, through reprinting in Western Europe and translation into English, has this precious little book become accessible to the wide circle interested in Russian religious life.

Nothing is known of the author. Written in the first person singular, the book presents itself as the spiritual autobiography of a Russian peasant who lived at about the middle of the nineteenth century, related in intimate conversations. The social conditions depicted in the story represent Russia during the last decades of serfdom, under the severe autocratic government of Nicholas I. The mention made of the Crimean War (1853–54) permits an exact chronological placement.

There are, however, many factors that do not allow us to accept literally the anonymous author's description of himself.

Although the style of the book has somewhat the flavor of the popular Russian idiom, it is essentially in the elaborate literary manner characteristic of the Russian spiritual writing of the middle of the nineteenth century. There are even many traces of the epoch of Alexandrian mysticism (Alexander I, 1801–1825) that deeply influenced the religious mentality and style of the Russian Church. Quite apart from the style, we come across many profound theological and philosophical digressions and comments that would be inconceivable in the mouth of a Russian peasant, even one well read in the *Philocalia*. The traces of a romanticism of Western origin are undeniable.

On the other hand, the many incidents related in detail, and even the confused order of the narrative, prevent us from dismissing the autobiographical form of the narration wholly as a literary convention. Probably a real experience of the pilgrim is the basis of the composition. Some educated person may have worked over the original oral confessions, either his actual "spiritual father," a priest or monk in Irkutsk (Siberia), or some monk on Mount Athos, whence the manuscript is supposed to have been brought to Kazan' by the abbot Païsius.

These critical remarks are intended to warn the reader not to accept the mystical life of the Pilgrim as reflecting Russian popular religion. On the contrary, it is the product of a fine spiritual culture, a rare flower in the Russian garden. Its main value consists in a convincingly detailed description of mental prayer as it was or could be practiced, not in a monastic cell, but by a layman, even under the peculiar conditions of a wandering life.

From another point of view, the book is a work of propaganda, designed to popularize in lay circles the mystical prayer of the Hesychasts as embodied in an ascetic-mystical anthology entitled the *Philocalia*. The first Greek edition of this anthology, the work of an anonymous compiler (probably Nicodemus of Mount Athos), was printed in Venice in 1782. The Slavonic translation by Païsius Velichkovsky was printed in 1793. Most of the Greek fathers of this collection were already known in Russia to Saint Nilus Sorsky in the fifteenth century. But from the sixteenth century onward, the mystical movement in Russia was suppressed until the time of the revival effected by Païsius. This Russian monk was an émigré living in the Balkan monasteries of Mount Athos and Rumania, where he imbibed the mystical tradition at its sources. The whole monastic revival that took form at the end of the eighteenth and the beginning of the nineteenth century in Russia is attributable to Païsius and his disciples. The Optina cloister in Russia (in the province of Kaluga), with its unbroken line of startzy, held itself to be the heir and depository in a special sense of Païsius's tradition.

That this tradition was not held within the confines of monasteries is demonstrated by the Pilgrim's book. It is his aim to convince us that mental prayer is possible in every condition of life. True, he admits that complete solitude is for him the most favorable condition for the practice of continual prayer: he often feels uneasy in human society when suddenly the Prayer of Jesus begins to "act of itself" in his heart. Yet the conditions under which a wanderer lives are as suitable for mystical prayer as is the cell of a monk.

The wandering life (this is a more correct English equivalent of the Russian phrase than "pilgrimage") is characteristic of Russian spirituality. Very often, as in the case of the present author, the wandering has no visit to a place of devotion as its object but is a way of life in which the early Christian ideal of spiritual freedom and detachment from the world is grafted on to the Russian feeling for the religious significance of nature as Mother Earth, and the truly Russian rejection of civilization out of religious motives. Yet, reading the tales of the Pilgrim, we realize that the mystical life of the author is moving against a background of the external manifestations of Christian charity. Some of his tales have little or nothing to do with the Prayer of Jesus, but portray ideal types of the evangelical life, found in all strata of society—among the gentry, the army, the clergy, the simple peasantry. These portraits of secular, uncanonized, and even unknown, lay saints are, as it were, a counterpoint to the scenes of cruelty, violence, and despotism that we are not spared. What is lacking is rather the average level of Russian life. The author has not the intention of depicting life around him as it is, but that of selecting instructive examples of Christian virtue.

A reader who would like to get a more adequate idea of Russian life under Nicholas I can be guided by many of the classical works of Russian literature: Gogol's *Dead Souls*, Turgenev's *Memoirs of a Sportsman*, the short stories of Leskov. The anonymous Pilgrim gives us rather exceptional specimens of Russian piety, authentic in themselves but inadequate as a basis for generalization.

The Way of a Pilgrim

Part One

By the grace of God I am a Christian, by my deeds a great sinner, and by calling a homeless rover of the lowest status in life. My possessions comprise but some rusk in a knapsack on my back, and the Holy Bible on my bosom. That is all.

On the twenty-fourth Sunday after Pentecost, I went to church to hear Mass. The first Epistle of Saint Paul to the Thessalonians was read. In it we are exhorted, among other things, to pray *incessantly,* and these words engraved themselves upon my mind. I began to ponder whether it is possible to pray without ceasing, since every man must occupy himself with other things needed for his support. I found this text in my Bible and read with my own eyes what I had heard, namely that we must pray incessantly in all places, pray always in spirit, lifting up our hands in devotion. I pondered and pondered and did not know what to think of it.

"What am I to do?" I mused. "Where will I be able to find someone who can explain it to me? I shall go to the churches known for their famous preachers; perhaps there I shall hear something that will enlighten me." And I went. I heard a great many very good sermons on prayer in general, how one ought to pray, what prayer is and what fruits it bears, but no one said how to succeed in it. There were sermons on spiritual prayer, on incessant prayer, but no one pointed out how it was to be accomplished.

Thus my attendance at the sermons failed to give me what I sought. Therefore, after having heard many of them, I gave them up without acquiring the desired knowledge of incessant prayer. I decided to look, with the help of God, for an experienced and learned man who would talk to me and explain the meaning of incessant prayer since the understanding of it seemed most important to me.

For a long time I went from one place to another, reading my Bible constantly, and inquiring everywhere whether there was not a spiritual teacher or a pious and experienced guide. Finally, I was informed that in a certain village there lived a gentleman who had, for many years, sought the salvation of his soul. He had a chapel in his house, never left the premises and spent his days praying and reading religious books. Upon hearing this I well-nigh ran to that particular village. I got there and went to the owner of the estate.

"What is it that you want?" he asked.

"I was told that you are a pious and intelligent man," I said. "For the love of God enlighten me in the meaning of the Apostle's utterance 'pray incessantly.' Is it possible for anyone to pray without ceasing? I wish I could know, but I do not seem to understand it at all."

The gentleman remained silent for a while, looking at me fixedly. Finally he said: "Incessant inner prayer is a continuous longing of the human spirit for God. But in order to succeed in this sweet practice we must pray more and ask God to teach us incessant prayer. Pray more and with fervor. It is prayer itself that will teach you how it can be done without ceasing; however, it will require some time."

Having said this he ordered that food be brought to me, gave me money for my journey and dismissed me. And in the end he had explained nothing at all.

Once more I set out. I pondered and pondered, read and read, and my thoughts dwelt constantly upon what this man had told me, though I could not understand what he meant. Yet, so ardently did I wish to fathom this question, that I could not sleep at night.

I traveled two hundred versts on foot and reached a large city that was the capital of the province. There I saw a monastery, and at the inn where I stayed I learned that the abbot was a kindly man, at once pious and hospitable. When I went to see him he received me in a friendly fashion, asked me to sit down and offered refreshments.

"Holy Father," I said, "I do not want any food, but I beg you, enlighten me in spiritual matters. Tell me how I can save my soul."

"How can you save your soul? Well, live according to the commandments, pray and you will be saved."

"But it is said that we should pray incessantly. I do not know how this can be done for I cannot even get the meaning of it. Father, I beseech you, explain to me what incessant prayer means."

"I do not know, dear brother, how to explain it to you! But wait a moment . . . I have a little book that will enlighten you," He handed me Saint Demetrius's[1] book, called *The Spiritual Education of the Inner Man* and said: "Here, read this page."

I read the following statement: "The words of the Apostle 'pray incessantly' should be interpreted as referring to the prayer of the mind, for the mind can always be soaring to God and pray without ceasing."

"But," I said, "won't you indicate to me the means by which the mind can always be directed to God without being disturbed in its incessant prayer?"

"This, indeed, is very difficult, unless God Himself bestows upon one such a gift," answered the abbot, and he offered no further explanations.

I spent the night in his monastery. The following morning I thanked him for his kind hospitality and went on my way, though I did not know myself where I was going. I was saddened by my incapacity to understand and read the Holy Bible for consolation.

In this wise I followed the main road for about five days when, one evening, I was overtaken by an elderly man who looked as though he belonged to the clergy. In reply to my question he answered that he was a monk from a monastery situated some ten versts off the main road and extended to me his invitation.

"In our guesthouse," he said, "we offer rest, shelter and food to pilgrims and other pious people." I did not care to go with him and replied that my peace of mind did not depend upon my lodging, but upon finding spiritual guidance. Neither was I concerned about my food, for I had a provision of rusk in my knapsack.

"What kind of spiritual guidance are you seeking? What is it that troubles you?" he asked. "Do come for a short stay, dear brother. We have experienced elders who will guide you and lead you to the true path in the light of the word of God and the teaching of the Holy Fathers."

I told him what was troubling me. The old man crossed himself and said: "Give thanks to God, my beloved brother, for he has awakened you to the irresistible longing for incessant, inner prayer. Acknowledge in it the voice of our Lord and be calm in the assurance that all that has happened to you hitherto was the testing of the compliance of your own will with the call of God. You have been given the privilege of understanding that the heavenly light of incessant inner prayer is not found in worldly wisdom or in mere striving for outward knowledge. On the contrary, it is attained in poverty of spirit, in active experience and in simplicity of heart. For this reason it is not astonishing that you have not been able to learn anything about the essential work of prayer or to attain the skill by which incessant activity in it is acquired. What is prayer and how does one learn to pray? Though these questions are vital and essential, one gets only rarely a true enlightenment on that subject from contemporary preachers. It is because these questions are more complex than all the arguments they have at their disposal. These questions require not merely academic achievements, but mystical insight. And one of the most lamentable things is the vanity of elementary knowledge that drives people to measure the Divine by a human yardstick. Only too often wrong reasoning is applied to prayer, for many believe that preparatory steps and great virtues lead us to prayer. In fact it is prayer that gives birth to all the virtues and sublime deeds. The fruits and consequences of prayer are wrongly taken for the means of attaining it. This attitude belittles the value of prayer, and it is contrary to the statements of the Holy Scripture. The Apostle Paul says: 'I desire therefore, first of all, that supplications be made.' Here the main thing that the Apostle stressed in his words about prayer is that prayer must come before anything else: 'I desire therefore, first of all' . . . There are many virtues that are required of a good Christian, but above all else he must pray; for nothing can ever be achieved without prayer. Otherwise he cannot find his way to God, he cannot grasp the truth, he cannot crucify the flesh with all its passions and desires, find the Light of Christ in his heart and be united to our Lord. Frequent prayer must precede all these things before they can be brought about. I say 'frequent' because the perfection and the correctness of prayer is beyond our power. 'For we know not what we should pray for as we ought,' says the Apostle Paul. Therefore we ought to pray often, to pray at all times, for this alone lies within our power and leads us to purity of prayer, which is the mother of all spiritual good. As Saint Isaac the Syrian says: 'Win the mother and she will bear you children,' so must you first of all attain the power of prayer, and then all other virtues will be easily practiced afterward. All this is scarcely mentioned by those who have had no personal experience, but only a superficial knowledge of the most mysterious teaching of the Holy Fathers."

While he talked to me, we reached the monastery without noticing it. In order that I might not lose contact with this wise elder, and to get further information more quickly, I hastened to say: "Reverend Father, do me a favor: Explain to me what incessant prayer is, and how I am to learn it. As I see, you are deeply versed in all these matters."

It was with kindness that he granted my request and taking me to his cell, he said: "Come in, I shall give you a book written by the Holy Fathers. With God's help you may get from it a clear and definite idea of what prayer is."

As we entered his cell he began to speak again: "The constant inner prayer of Jesus is an unbroken, perpetual calling upon the Divine Name of Jesus with the lips, the mind and the heart, while picturing His lasting presence in one's imagination and imploring His grace wherever one is, in whatever one does, even while one sleeps. This prayer consists of the following words: 'Lord Jesus Christ, have mercy on me!' Those who use this prayer constantly are so greatly comforted that they are moved to say it at all times, for they can no longer live without it. And the prayer will keep on ringing in their hearts of its own accord. Now, do you understand what incessant prayer is?"

"Yes, I do, Father. In the Name of God explain to me how to achieve the mastery of it," I said, feeling overwhelmed with joy.

"You will learn how to master it by reading this book, which is called the *Philocalia;* it comprises the complete and minute knowledge of incessant inner prayer, as stated by twenty-five Holy Fathers. It is full of great wisdom and is so useful that it is regarded as the first and best guide by all those who seek the contemplative, spiritual life. The reverend Nicephorus said once: 'It leads one to salvation without labor and sweat.'"

"Is it then loftier and holier than the Bible?" I asked.

"No, it is not, but it sheds light upon the secrets locked up in the Bible that cannot be easily understood by our shallow intelligence. Let me give you an analogy: the largest, the brightest and at the same time the most wonderful of all luminaries is the sun; yet you must protect your eyes in order to examine it, or simply to look at it. For this purpose you use artificial glass, millions and millions of times smaller and darker than the sun. But through this tiny piece of glass you can contemplate the sublime king of all stars with its flamboyant rays. Thus the Holy Scripture is like the resplendent sun, while this book—the *Philocalia*—may be compared to the piece of glass that permits us to contemplate its lofty magnificence. Now, listen; I shall read you the instructions on incessant prayer as they are given here."

He opened the book, and after having found the instruction by Saint Simeon the New Theologian, he began to read: "Take a seat in solitude and silence. Bend your head, close your eyes, and breathing softly, in your imagination, look into your own heart. Let your mind, or rather, your thoughts, flow from your head down to your heart and say, while breathing: 'Lord Jesus Christ, have mercy on me.' Whisper these words gently, or say them in your mind. Discard all other thoughts. Be serene, persevering and repeat them over and over again."

The elder did not limit himself to mere explanations, but made them clear by examples. We read passages of Saint Gregory of Sinai, Saint Callistus and Saint Ignatius[2] and he interpreted them to me in his own words. I listened to him attentively, overwhelmed with gladness, and did my best to store every detail in my memory. Thus we stayed up the whole night together and went to Matins without having slept at all.

When the elder dismissed me with his blessings, he told me that while I was learning the ways of prayer I must return and relate to him my experiences in a full and sincere confession; for this work cannot be crowned with success except with the attentive guidance of a teacher.

In the church I felt a burning zeal to practice incessant prayer diligently and asked God to help me. Then I began to ask myself how I could visit the elder for guidance and confession, since it was not permitted to remain in the monastery guesthouse for more than three days, and there were no other houses nearby.

However, I soon discovered a village situated about four versts from the monastery. When I went there in search of living quarters, God led me to the right place. A peasant engaged me for the whole summer to take care of his kitchen garden; he placed at my disposal a hut where I could live by myself. Praise be to God! I came upon a quiet place! I took up my dwelling and began to learn inner prayer in the manner I had been told and went to see my elder from time to time.

Alone in my garden, I practiced incessant prayer for a week as the elder had directed me. In the beginning things went very well. But soon I began to feel tired, lazy and bored. Overcome by drowsiness, I was often distracted by all kinds of thoughts that came upon me like a cloud. I went to see my elder in great anxiety and told him of my plight.

He received me cordially and said: "The kingdom of darkness assails you, my dear brother. To it nothing is worse than a prayer of the heart. And the kingdom of darkness uses every means at its disposal to hold you back and to prevent you from learning prayer. Nevertheless the fiend can do no more than God will permit, no more than is needed for our own good. It seems that your humility needs more testing; it is too soon for you to approach with intemperate zeal the sublime entrance of the heart, lest you fall into spiritual covetousness. Let me read you an instruction from the *Philocalia* about this case."

The elder found the teaching of Nicephorus the monk, and began to read: "If after some efforts you do not succeed in reaching the region of the heart in the manner you have been told, do what I am about to tell you, and with the help of God you will find what you are seeking. The faculty of speech is located in the larynx, as you know. Drive backs all other thoughts—you can do it if you wish—and use that faculty in saying constantly the following words: 'Lord Jesus Christ, have mercy on me.' Make yourself do so at all times. If you persist in it for a while, your heart by this means will be open to prayer without doubt. This is known from experience."

"Here you have the teaching of Holy Fathers dealing with these cases," said the elder. "Therefore you must accept it with confidence and repeat the oral Jesus Prayer as often as possible. Take this rosary. Use it in saying three thousand prayers every day in the beginning. Whether you sit or stand, walk or lie down, constantly repeat: 'Lord Jesus Christ, have mercy on me.' Do it quietly, without hurrying, but say it exactly three thousand times a day, neither increasing nor diminishing the number of prayers of your own accord. By this means God will help you to attain also the incessant action of the heart."

With joy I accepted this instruction and returned to my lodging, where I began to carry out faithfully and exactly what the elder ordered me to do. It was somewhat hard for two days. Later it became so easy and pleasant that I felt something like a longing for the prayer; I said it willingly and cheerfully, and not under compulsion as before.

I told my elder of this and he decreed that I recite six thousand prayers a day: "Be calm," he admonished me, "and try to say as faithfully as possible the fixed number of prayers. The Lord in His mercy will give you His grace."

In my solitary hut I said for a whole week the Jesus Prayer six thousand times a day, forgetting all cares and discarding all other thoughts, however much they assailed me. I had in mind but the one aim of fulfilling the bidding of the elder faithfully. And, behold! I got so used to my prayer that when I stopped for a short time I felt as if I was missing something, as if I had undergone a loss. And the minute I started it all over again I had the joyous sensation of freedom. When I met people, I did not care to enter into conversation at all, for all I desired was to be left alone and to say my prayer, so accustomed had I grown to it during that week.

The elder, who had not seen me for about ten days, called on me himself. I told him how I was getting along. He listened attentively and then said: "Now that you have become accustomed to prayer, persist in this habit and strengthen it. Waste no time, and with the help of God say precisely twelve thousand prayers a day from now on. Keep to yourself, get up early, go to bed later than usual, and come to me for advice twice a month."

I did as the elder ordered me to do. On the first day I had barely finished my twelve thousand prayers by the late evening. But the following day they flowed with greater ease and joy. At first the incessant saying of the prayer wearied me to a certain extent; my tongue was somewhat numbed and my jaws stiff. My palate, too, hurt a little, but this was not unpleasant at all. I felt a slight pain in the thumb of my left hand, which I used for counting my beads. A minor inflammation developed in my left arm from the wrist up to the elbow. The sensation it caused was most pleasant; it stimulated and urged me to the frequent saying of the prayer. Thus for about five days I said faithfully my twelve thousand prayers, and as the habit became fixed I did it willingly and with joy.

Early one morning I was, so to speak, aroused by the prayer. When I began to recite my morning prayers, my tongue refused to utter the familiar words with ease. My only desire was to go on with the Jesus Prayer, and no sooner had I started it than I felt joyfully relieved. My lips and my tongue recited the words without any effort on my part. I spent the whole day experiencing great happiness and a complete detachment from earthly things, as though I were living on another planet. Easily did I finish my twelve thousand prayers by the early evening. I wished I might keep on, but I dared not to increase the number fixed by my elder. The following day I continued in the same way, calling on the name of Jesus Christ, and did it with readiness and facility. Then I went to see the elder and, opening my heart, I told him everything in detail.

He listened to me attentively and then began to speak: "Thank God for having discovered in yourself the desire and facility for prayer. This is a natural result that crowns continuous efforts and action. It is like this: a machine operates for a while if its principal wheel is given a push; however, if it is to operate still longer, that wheel must be oiled and given another push.

And so is the sensual nature of man, which God in His loving mercy has endowed with great capacities. You have yourself experienced what a feeling can be born in a sinful soul not yet in the state of grace, not yet purified from all sensuality. But how comforting, wonderful and sublime it is when God in His benevolence cleanses the soul of man from passion and bestows upon him the gift of self-acting, spiritual prayer! This state is impossible to describe, for the revelation of the mystery of prayer foretells here on earth the bliss of heaven. That kind of happiness is granted to loving hearts that seek after God in simplicity. Now I authorize you to recite the prayer as often as you wish, the more the better. Give it all your waking hours, and from now on call on the name of Jesus without counting. Submit yourself to the will of God in humility, looking to Him for assistance. I firmly believe that He will not abandon you but direct your steps."

Following these instructions I spent the whole summer in incessant oral prayer to Jesus, enjoying peace of mind and soul. I often dreamed in my sleep that I was reciting the prayer. If during the day I happened to meet people, I felt that I liked them as though they were my closest relatives, but I wasted none of my time on them. My thoughts calmed down by themselves. I was concerned with nothing but my prayer, to which my mind was beginning to listen; and from time to time the sensation of delightful warmth was sweeping over my heart. Whenever I went to church the long monastic services seemed short to me and failed to tire me out as had happened before.

And my lonely hut had for me all the splendor of a palace. I did not know how to thank God for having guided me, a miserable sinner, to that saving elder who became my master.

However, I was not long to profit by the instructions of my beloved teacher, who was blessed with divine wisdom. At the end of the summer he passed away. I bade him my last farewell in tears and in profound gratitude for the fatherly guidance he had given to a poor wretch like myself. For a blessing I begged permission to keep the rosary that he had been using in his prayers.

Thus I remained alone. Summer passed and the work in the kitchen garden came to an end. My peasant dismissed me, giving me two rubles for my work as a watchman and filling up my knapsack with rusk for my journey. Once more I set off on my wanderings to various places. But now I was no longer alone and in want as before. Calling upon the Name of Jesus brought cheer to me on my way. People I met were kind to me as if they liked me.

Thus I began to wonder what to do with the money I had earned for my work in the kitchen garden. What was it good for? "Look here," I said to myself. My elder was gone. I had no one to guide me. Why not buy the *Philocalia* with the purpose of learning from it more about inner prayer.

I made the sign of the cross and went on my way reciting my prayer. When I came to a large province town I began to look for the *Philocalia* in all the stores. Finally I found the book, but they asked me three rubles for it, whereas I had only two in my possession. I haggled and haggled over the price, but the shopkeeper would not give in. In the end he suggested: "Go to that church nearby and speak to the warden. He has a very old copy of this book and may be willing to sell it to you for two rubles." I made my way there and lo! for my two rubles I bought the *Philocalia*. It was an old copy, much damaged by use. Overjoyed with my purchase, I repaired it as well as I could, made a cloth cover for it, and put it into my knapsack with the Bible.

And now, I am wandering about repeating incessantly the Prayer of Jesus. To me it has greater value than anything else on earth. Occasionally I walk seventy versts or so and do not feel it at all. I am conscious of only one thing, my prayer. When bitter cold pierces me, I say it more eagerly and warm up in no time. When I am hungry I begin to call on the Name of Jesus more often and forget about food. When I am ill and rheumatic pains set in in my back and legs, I concentrate on the prayer and no longer notice the discomfort. When people do me wrong, my wrath and indignation are quickly forgotten as soon as I remember the sweetness of the Prayer of Jesus. In a way I have become a half-witted person; I have no anxiety and no interest in the vanities of the world, for which I care no longer. I am longing by habit for only one thing, to be left alone and to pray incessantly. When I am doing this I am filled with joy. God knows what is going on within me. It is sensuous, no doubt! As my departed elder explained to me, this is natural and artificial at the same time, as a consequence of my daily practice. But I realize my lack of merit and of intelligence and dare not proceed further in learning and mastering the spiritual prayer within my heart. God will enlighten me at the same time. Meanwhile, I hope that my late elder prays for me. Though I have not yet reached the state in which ceaseless spiritual prayer is self-acting in the heart, I do understand, thank God, the meaning of the Apostle's words in the Epistle: "Pray incessantly."

Part Two

I ROAMED ABOUT through many different places for a long time with the Prayer of Jesus as my sole companion. It gladdened and comforted me in all my wanderings, my meetings with other people and in all the incidents of the journey. Soon, however, it occurred to me that it would be better to take a fixed abode so as to be alone more often and study the *Philocalia* more easily. Though I read this book whenever I could in all the refuges I was able to find for the night's or day's rest, I felt that I ought to dedicate more time to it. With faith and concentration I wished to gather from its instruction more information about the truth that would save my soul by means of inner prayer.

But despite my sincere desire I could not find any work whatever, for my left arm was crippled from early childhood. Because of this I was not able to make a permanent home for myself. Thus I made up my mind to go to Siberia and to visit the tomb of Saint Innocent in Irkutsk.[3] I thought that I would travel in the great silence of Siberian forests and steppes in a manner that was more suitable for praying and reading. I set off and on my way recited the prayer without ceasing.

At the end of a short period I began to feel that the prayer had, so to speak, passed to my heart. In other words I felt that my heart in its natural beating began, as it were, to utter the words of the prayer. For instance, *one* "Lord"; *two* "Jesus"; *three* "Christ," and so forth. No longer did I say the prayer with my lips, but listened attentively to the words formed in my heart, remembering what my departed elder told me about this state of bliss. Then I began to feel a slight pain in my heart, and my whole being was glowing with so great a love for Jesus Christ that it seemed to me if only I could meet Him, I would fall to His feet, embracing them and kissing them in tenderness, tears and gratitude for His love and mercy, which gives such comfort in calling on His Name to me, His unworthy creature. A pleasant warmth was filling my heart and spreading through my whole bosom. This urged me to a more eager reading of the *Philocalia,* so as to test my emotions and to study further the effects of inner prayer. Without this test I might have fallen a victim of delusion, or might have taken natural results for the manifestation of grace, and prided myself at the quick mastering of the prayer. My late elder had warned me of this danger. I decided therefore to walk more at night and to devote my days mainly to reading the *Philocalia,* sitting under the forest trees. Ah! A wisdom so great that I had never thought it possible was revealed to me in this reading. As I went on, I felt a happiness that, until then, had been beyond my imagination.

Although many passages were still incomprehensible to my dull mind, the Prayer of the Heart brought the understanding I wanted. Besides, on rare occasions, I dreamed of my late elder, who explained many things to me, and, above all, led my dormant soul to the path of humility.

Thus, blissfully happy, I spent more than two months of the summer. As a general rule I made my way through the forest, choosing byways. Whenever I entered a village I asked only for rusk and a little salt. With my bark jar filled with water I made another hundred versts.

Summer was drawing to a close as I was assailed with trials and temptations. Were they the consequence of sins weighing on my wretched soul? Or was something lacking in my spiritual life that required other experiences? I do not know. This is what happened: One day, at twilight, when I reached the main road, two men looking like soldiers caught up with me and demanded money. When I told them that I had not a penny on me, they refused to believe me and shouted rudely: "You are lying. Pilgrims always collect plenty of money."

"What is the use of talking to him," said one of them, and he hit me on the head with his club with such force that I fell senseless to the ground. How long I remained unconscious I do not know, but when I came to myself I was lying by the forest road, robbed. My knapsack was gone from my back; only the cords that had fastened it and which they had cut, remained. Thank God! they had not taken my passport, for I kept it in my old cap, ready to show it at a moment's notice. I rose, shedding bitter tears, not so much on account of the pain in my head, as for the loss of the Bible and the *Philocalia*, which were in the stolen bag.

I did not cease to mourn and to wail day and night. Where was my Bible, which I had carried with me all this time and read since my early youth? Where was my *Philocalia*, which gave me so much enlightenment and consolation? Alas, I had lost my first and last treasures in life without having enjoyed them fully. It would have been better for me to have been killed on the spot, than to exist without spiritual food. There was no way of replacing these books now.

Heavily I dragged myself for two days, overcome by my calamity. Exhausted at the end of the third day, I fell to the ground and went to sleep in the shelter of a bush. And then I had a dream. I saw myself in the monastery cell of my elder, lamenting over my loss. In his endeavor to console me the old man was saying: "You must learn therefrom detachment from worldly things for your greater progress toward heaven. All this has been allowed to come to pass so as to prevent you from slipping into mere enjoyment of spiritual sweetness. God wills that a Christian relinquish his desires, his attachments and his own will, so as to give himself entirely to the Divine Providence. God directs all events for the good of mankind, for 'He wills that all men should be saved.' Be of good cheer and trust that along with the temptation God provides also a way of escape. In a short time you will rejoice more than you grieve now."

As these words were spoken, I woke up, my strength returned and my soul was at peace, as though filled with the brightness of dawn. "God's will be done," I said, and, crossing myself, got up and went on my way. Once more the prayer was self-acting in my heart as it had been before, and I walked serenely for three days.

All of a sudden I met a group of convicts escorted by soldiers. When I came closer I saw the two men who had robbed me. As they were in the outside row, I fell to their feet and asked them urgently to tell me where my books were. In the beginning they paid no attention to my plea; finally one of them said: "If you'll give us something, we'll tell you where your books are. Give us a ruble."

I swore that I would gladly give them a ruble, even if I had to beg it for the love of God, and offered to leave with them my passport in pawn. At this, they told me that my books might be found in one of the carriages that followed the convicts with other stolen things, which had been found on them.

"Well, but how can I get them?"

"Speak to the officer in charge."

I rushed to the officer and told him what had happened.

"Do you mean to say that you can read the Bible?" he asked.

"Indeed, I can," I replied. "Not only can I read everything, but I can also write. You will see my name written on the Bible, which proves that it belongs to me. And here is my passport bearing the same name and surname."

The officer told me that the two villains were deserters and lived in a forest hut. They had plundered many people until a quick-witted driver, whose *troika* they were about to steal, had caught them the day before. "Very well," he added, "I will return your books if they are there, but won't you walk with us as far as our stopping place for the night? It will save me from halting men and carriages on your account." I willingly agreed to this, and while I walked at the side of his horse, we fell into conversation.

The officer impressed me as being a kind and upright man, no longer young. He wished to know who I was, where I came from and where I was planning to go. To all his questions I gave a frank reply, and so we came to the house that marked the journey's end for that day. The officer got my books, and, returning them to me, said: "Now that it is night, stay here; you may sleep in my entrance-hall." I stayed.

I was so happy to have my books again that I did not know how to thank God. I pressed them to my chest for such a long time that my hands got quite stiff. I wept from exultation, my heart beating with gladness. The officer looked at me fixedly and said: "I see that you are very fond of your Bible." My happiness was so great that I was not able to speak. He continued: "I, too, read the Gospel every day, brother." He took from his breast pocket a small book of the Gospels bound in silver. It was printed in Kiev. "Take a seat," he said. "Let me tell you what happened to me."

"Hey, there! bring us some supper," he ordered.

We sat down to the table and the officer told me his story.

I have been in the army since my early youth—not in a garrison, but in the field service. My superiors liked me, for I knew my business and fulfilled my duties as a second lieutenant conscientiously. But I was young and had many friends. Unfortunately, I took to the bottle so that my passion became a disease. As long as I remained sober, I was a reliable officer, but when I yielded to temptation I was good for nothing, sometimes for a period of six weeks. They stood me for a long time, but in the end, when, in a state of intoxication, I insulted my commanding officer, I was degraded and transferred to a garrison as a private soldier for three years. And I was warned that a still more severe punishment was in store for me if I did not reform and give up drinking. I was so miserable that all my efforts to control or to cure myself proved vain. When I was told that I was to be sent to prison, I did not know what to do with myself. As I sat in the barracks plunged in my bitter thoughts, a monk came in. He was making a collection for a church. We gave him what we could.

The monk approached me and asked why I looked so sad. We began to talk and I told him of my misery. He said compassionately: "My brother had the same experience. And what do you suppose has cured him? His spiritual father provided him with a copy of the Gospels and bade him to read a chapter as soon as he felt the urge to drink. If it persisted he was told to read the second chapter, and so forth. My brother did so, and before long he stopped drinking altogether. Now, for fifteen years he has never touched as much as a drop of alcohol. Won't you try the same cure? You'll see that it will help you. I have a copy of the Gospels and will bring it to you."

I listened to him and said: "How can your Gospels help me when my own efforts and medical treatment have failed to stop me from drinking?" I spoke in that way because I never read the Gospels.

"Don't say that," answered the monk. "I am sure it will help you." And he brought me this very book the following day. As I glanced at it and tried to read a little, I said to the monk: "No, I won't take it. I can't understand it and I am not familiar with Church Slavonic." The monk, however, insisted that there is a grace-giving power in the words of the Gospels, for they relate what our Lord Himself had said. "It is unimportant if you do not understand; just go on reading," he urged me. "A saint said once upon a time: 'you may not understand the Word of God, but the devils do, and tremble.' And the poison of drunkenness is, certainly, incited by devils. Let me tell you another thing: Saint John Chrysostom writes that even a lodging in which there is a Gospel wards off the spirits of darkness, for it proves to be a wrong place for their deceiving tricks."

I forget how much money I gave the monk, but in the end I took his Gospel, packed it into my trunk with my other belongings and did not give it another thought. Sometime later when I was overcome by an insurmountable urge to drink, I opened my trunk hastily, so as to take out some money and dash to a tavern. Then I saw the book of the Gospels and the words of the monk came back to my mind. I came across a chapter of Saint Matthew and began to read; though I did not understand a word of it, I finished it remembering what the monk had said: "It is unimportant if you do not understand, just go on reading."

"Well," I said to myself, "I will read the second chapter." As I did so, I realized that I understood it somewhat better. So I began reading the third chapter, until the barracks bell rang the signal for retreat, after which no one was permitted to go out. So I stayed where I was.

The following morning, upon rising, I was just about to get myself a drink when I thought of reading another chapter of the Gospels. What was the result of it? Well, I read and did not go to the tavern. As soon as I craved a drink I read a chapter and felt somewhat relieved. This gave me confidence, and from that time on, whenever I felt like drinking, I resorted to the Gospels. Things improved greatly in a while. When I had finished the four Gospels my drunkenness was completely gone. I felt nothing but disgust for alcohol and for twenty years have never tasted a drop of it.

I was so greatly changed that everyone noticed it with surprise. Three years later my commission was restored to me. In due time I got a promotion and finally rose to the rank of a captain. I am married. My wife is a good woman. We are well provided for and live comfortably, thank God! We help the poor as far as our means permit and shelter the pilgrims. My son is also an officer now—a good boy. Note this, after I was cured of alcoholism, I vowed to read the Gospels every day as long as I lived—one Gospel in every twenty-four hours, allowing nothing to stop me from doing it. When I am very busy and too tired to do it myself, I relax and ask my wife or my son to read one Gospel to me, so that I may avoid breaking my vow.

I ordered a binding of pure silver for this copy of the Gospels. This I did for the glory of God and by way of thanksgiving, and I keep it constantly on my breast.

I listened to the Captain's story with pleasure and said: "I also happen to know a similar case. There was a workman at our village factory, a nice fellow, very clever at his work. Unfortunately he used to drink, and not infrequently. A certain God-fearing man had suggested that whenever a craving for alcohol gripped him he should recite the Prayer of Jesus thirty-three times for the glory of the Holy Trinity and in remembrance of the thirty-three years of the earthly life of Jesus Christ. The workman paid heed to this advice and carried it out. In a short while he was no longer drinking at all. And what is more, he entered a monastery three years later."

"Which do you think is best?" asked the captain, "the Prayer of Jesus or the Gospels?"

"It is quite the same thing," I answered. "What the Gospel is, so is the Prayer of Jesus, for the Divine Name of Jesus Christ contains all the truth of the Gospel. The Holy Fathers tell us that the Prayer of Jesus summarizes the whole Gospel."

We set out to say the prayers after our conversation. The Captain started on the Gospel of Saint Mark from the beginning. I listened to it and recited the prayer in my heart. After one o'clock in the morning he finished his reading and we retired to rest.

I got up at daybreak as usual, when everybody was still asleep. When it began to dawn I got hold of my beloved *Philocalia*. With what joy I opened it! It was as though I had seen my own father returning from a distant land, or a dead friend who had just risen. I covered it with my kisses, thanking God for having returned it to me. Wasting no time, I opened the second part of the book and began to read Theoliptus of Philadelphia. His instructions startled me, for he suggests that one and the same person do three different things at once. "Seated at the table, give nourishment to your body, fill your ears with reading and your mind with prayer." But when I remembered the happy evening I had spent the day before, I understood from my own experience what was the real meaning of this thought. And here I got the revelation that mind and heart are not one and the same thing.

When the Captain rose I went to bid him farewell and to thank him for his kindness. He treated me to tea, gave me a ruble and said goodbye. Joyfully, I started on my way. I had gone scarcely a verst, when I recalled that I had promised to give the soldiers a ruble, which had come into my possession in an unexpected way. At first I wondered whether I should give it to them or not. After all, they had beaten me and robbed me; besides, money would be of no use to them since they were under arrest. Then another thought coursed through my mind. I remembered what the Bible says: "If thy enemy be hungry, give him to eat." And Jesus Christ bade us "to love our enemies"; and "if any man will take away thy coat let him have thy cloak also." Thus, the question was settled in my mind. I retraced my steps and came just in time, when the prisoners were about to start on their march. Quickly I approached one of the soldiers and slipped the ruble into his hands, saying: "Repent and pray. Jesus Christ is merciful. He will not forsake you." I left them with these words and went on my way in another direction.

I walked for some fifty versts along the high road. Then I decided to take a side-road so as to be alone and read in peace. I was going through a dense forest for a long time. Only rarely did I come upon even small villages. Occasionally I would spend nearly a whole day sitting in the forest and attentively reading the *Philocalia*, which to me was an inexhaustible source of knowledge. There was in my heart a burning desire to unite with God by means of inner prayer, and I was anxious to learn it, using my book as a guide. I could not help regretting that I had no abode where I could read in peace all the time.

Meanwhile I was also reading my Bible and became aware of a clearer understanding of it than before, when I had failed to grasp a multitude of things and had many perplexities. The Holy Fathers were right in their assertion that the *Philocalia* represents a key to the mysteries of the Scripture. It helped me to understand, to a certain degree, the Word of God in its hidden meaning. I began to perceive the significance of the following sayings: "The inner secret man of the heart," "true prayer," "worships in the spirit," "the kingdom of God within us," "the intercession of the Holy Spirit with unspeakable groanings," "abide in Me," "give Me thy heart," "to put on Christ," "the betrothal of the Spirit to our hearts," the cry from the depths of the heart, "Abba, Father," and so forth. And when I prayed in my heart bearing all this in mind, everything about me appeared to be pleasing and lovely. It was as though the trees, the grass, the birds, the earth, the air and the light were saying that they existed for the sake of man, in testimony and proof of the love of God for mankind. It was as if they were saying that everything prayed and praised God.

In this manner I began to get the meaning of what the *Philocalia* describes as "the understanding of the language of the creation" and I saw that there were ways of conversing with all the creatures of God.

Thus I wandered about for a long time. Finally I came to a district so isolated that for three days I saw no villages at all. My provision of rusk was exhausted, and I was disheartened at the thought that I might perish from hunger. Then I prayed in my heart, entrusting myself to the divine will, and my anxiety left me at once. My mind was at peace again and I regained my good spirits. As I walked farther along the road bordered by a vast forest, a dog ran out of it and trotted in front of me.

When I called him, he came up to me in a friendly fashion. I was very happy at the thought that this was another proof of God's mercy. Surely there was a flock grazing in the forest and this dog belonged to the shepherd. There was also a possibility that a hunter was in the neighborhood. At any rate I would be able to ask for bread, if nothing else, for I had gone without food for twenty-four hours. At least they would be able to tell me where the nearest village was.

The dog jumped around me for a while, but seeing that I was not going to give him anything, he ran back to the narrow path by which he had come. I had followed him for a few hundred yards among the trees when I noticed that he ran into a burrow, looked out and barked. And then out from behind a large tree came a middle-aged peasant, gaunt and pale. He wanted to know where I came from: In my turn, I asked him what he was doing there, and a friendly conversation began. The peasant invited me to his hut, explaining that he was a forester in charge of this particular section, which had been sold for timber. As he placed bread and salt in front of me, we began to talk once more. "I just envy you," I said. "Aren't you lucky to live here quietly, all by yourself. Look at me, I ramble from place to place and rub shoulders with all kinds of people."

"You may stay here if you wish to," he said. "The old dugout of the former forester is not far from here. It is in bad condition, but still good enough to live in in summer. You have your passport. Don't worry about bread; we shall have enough for both of us. My village supplies me with it every week. This little brook here never dries up. This is all I need, brother. For the past ten years I have lived on bread only and drunk nothing but water. That's how it goes. In the fall, when the farmers have finished tilling the land, some two hundred workers will come to fell these trees. Then my business here will come to an end, and you will not be permitted to remain either."

As I heard all this I well-nigh fell to his feet from sheer joy. I knew not how to thank God for His mercy. My greatest desire was fulfilled in this unexpected way. There were still over four months at my disposal before the next fall. And during that time I could give myself to attentive reading of the *Philocalia* in my endeavor to study and to master the incessant Prayer of the Heart. Thus, I stayed there with joy and lived in the dugout he had shown me.

I often talked with this simple-hearted brother who had sheltered me, and he told me the story of his life and of his thoughts.

"I enjoyed a good position in our village," he said. "I owned a workshop where I dyed red and blue linens. My life was easy but not without sin. I cheated, swore in vain, used foul language, drank to excess and quarreled with my neighbors. There lived in our village an old church-reader who had an ancient book on the Last Judgment. He used to go from house to house reading from it and thus earning a few pennies. Occasionally he would come to me. For ten kopeks he would read all night long till cockcrow. While working, I often listened to his reading about the torments of Hell, about the living who will be changed and the dead who will rise from their graves, about God who will judge the world with the angels sounding their trumpets. I learned about fire and pitch and the worms that will eat up sinners. One day as I listened I was overcome by horror at the thought that these torments might be in store for me. Stop! I decided to work for the salvation of my soul, hoping that I would be able to pray my sins away. I pondered over the whole matter, then I quit my work; and since I was all alone in the world, I sold my house and took the job of forester here. All I ask of the village assembly is bread, a few clothes and candles for my prayers. I have lived in this manner for over ten years. I eat once a day and my meal consists of bread and water only. I get up with the roosters, make my morning devotions, burn the seven candles in front of the holy icons and pray. When I make my round in the forest I wear sixty pounds of iron chains under my clothes. I never use bad language, never drink wine or beer and no longer come to blows. As for women and girls, I have been avoiding them all my life.

"At first I was very pleased with my existence, but now other thoughts begin to assail me, and I cannot be rid of them. Only God knows whether I will be able to atone for my sins in this way. And my life is hard. I cannot help wondering if everything written in that book is true? Is it possible for the dead to rise again? And what if a man has been dead for over a hundred years, and even his ashes exist no longer? Who can tell whether there is a Hell or not? Why, no one has returned from the Beyond! It seems that when a man dies and rots, he is gone forever. That book might have been written by priests and lords so as to frighten us poor fools, and keep us quiet. Perhaps we torment ourselves in vain and forsake our pleasures and happiness for nothing at all. What then, if there is no such thing as an afterlife? Would it not be better to enjoy what we have on earth and take things easy? I am often disturbed by such thoughts now. I don't know. Maybe some day I shall return to my former work."

I listened to him with compassion. They say, I thought, that only educated and intelligent men have no faith whatever. Well, here was one of ourselves, an ordinary peasant, and what impious thoughts he had! It looks as if the kingdom of darkness finds access to everyone, and perhaps the simple-minded are its easiest prey. Let us seek wisdom and strength in the Word of God and brace ourselves for the fight with the enemy of our souls.

It was my sincere desire to help this brother in strengthening his faith. With this intention I took the *Philocalia* out of my knapsack, opened it and read to him the 109th chapter of Saint Hesychius. I tried to explain that it was worthless and vain to keep away from sin merely from fear of Hell and told him that the only way to relieve our souls from sinful thoughts is to guard our mind and purify our hearts by means of inner prayer. The Holy Fathers tell us that those who seek salvation from the mere fear of Hell are regarded as slaves, and those who perform glorious deeds in order to be rewarded with the Kingdom of Heaven are simply mercenary. God wills us to come to him in the manner of sons. He wishes us to lead honorable lives for the love of Him and from the eagerness to serve Him. He wishes us to seek felicity in uniting ourselves to Him in mind and heart.

"However difficult may be the physical tasks, which you impose upon your body, it is a wrong way to strive for peace," I said. "Without God in your mind and the incessant Prayer of Jesus in your heart, you are almost certain to slip back into sin on the slightest provocation. Start to work, brother, make up your mind to say the Jesus Prayer incessantly. You have here, in this remote place, a unique opportunity to do it. And you will profit by it in a short time. Godless thoughts will assail you no longer. The faith and the love of Jesus Christ will be revealed to you. You will be given to understand how the dead rise and what the Last Judgment is in reality. You will be amazed at the sense of lightness and bliss that follows the prayer. Boredom will fade away and will not trouble your solitary life."

Then I began to explain as well as I could how one is to proceed with the incessant prayer of Jesus, what is said about it in the Word of God and in the instructions of the Holy Fathers. He seemed to compose himself and to agree with me.

After this we separated and I locked myself in the old dugout he had given me. Almighty God! How happy and calm I was when I crossed the threshold of my cave, which looked more like a tomb. To me it was a splendid royal palace filled with comfort and delight. Shedding tears of joy I offered thanksgiving to God and thought that in this peaceful and quiet place I must start to work at my task and beg God for enlightenment. So, once more I began to read the *Philocalia* from the first page to the end, with great attention. Before long I had finished the entire book and realized how much wisdom, sanctity and profound insight it contained. But it dealt with such a vast variety of subjects and so many instructions of the Holy Fathers that it was beyond me to understand all and to summarize all I wished to know, particularly about inner prayer. Yet I ardently longed for it, in accordance with the divine bidding in the words of the Apostle: "Be zealous for the better gifts," and further, "extinguish not the Spirit." I pondered over it for a long time. What was I to do? The task was beyond my reason and my understanding, and there was no one who could have explained it to me—I resolved to beset the Lord with my prayer. He could enlighten me somehow or other. And for twenty-four hours I did nothing but pray, without ceasing for a moment. At last my thoughts stilled and I fell asleep.

I dreamed that I was in the cell of my departed elder who was explaining the *Philocalia* to me. He was saying: "There is a deep wisdom in this holy book. It is the hidden treasury of the meanings of the mysterious ways of God. The access to this treasury is not revealed everywhere and to everybody. And the guidance given here is subordinated to individual needs: the wise receives from it a subtle guidance, the plain man a simple one. Therefore you, simple-minded, must not read the chapters in succession as they appear in this book. It was meant for those who are versed in theology. Those who are not thus instructed but wish to learn inner prayer, should read the *Philocalia* in the following order: (1) the book of Nicephorus the Monk (part two must be read first of all); (2) then take the entire book of Gregory of Sinai, leaving out the short chapters; (3) read the Three Forms of Prayer by Simeon the New Theologian and his sermon on Faith; (4) then comes the book of Callistus and Ignatius. These Fathers give full guidance and instruction in the inner Prayer of the Heart, couched in words accessible to everyone. If you desire a still clearer understanding of prayer, open part four and read of the way of prayer as it was summarized by the most holy Callistus,[4] Patriarch of Constantinople."

In my dream, still holding the book in my hand, I was trying to find this particular instruction but failed. Then the elder went through a few pages himself, saying, "Here it is. Let me mark it for you." And with a piece of charcoal picked up from the floor he indicated with a mark on the margin the chapter he had found. I listened to him carefully, trying to remember, word for word, what he had been saying.

It was still dark when I woke up. I lay quietly thinking of my dream and of the words of my elder. "God alone knows,"

I said to myself, "whether I have really seen the spirit of my departed teacher or only imagined it in my mind, for it is constantly riveted on the *Philocalia* and on him." Prey to this doubt, I rose at daybreak. And behold! The book lay on a stone, which I used as a table in my dugout; it was open at the very page that my elder had indicated to me, with the charcoal mark on the margin, just as I had seen it in my dream. And the charcoal lay next to the book. I looked in amazement, for the book had not been there the evening before. On that point my recollection was clear; I had closed it and slipped it under my pillow; neither had there been the charcoal on it. I was quite sure of that too.

This strengthened me in my belief that my dream was true and that my beloved teacher of blessed memory was agreeable to the Lord. I started to read the *Philocalia* just as he had bidden me to do. I read it once, then again, and my soul was aroused by an ardent longing to experience in practice what I have been reading about. Now I understood clearly the meaning of inner prayer, how it may be attained and what the fruits of it are. I also was given to see how it filled the heart with sweetness and how one was to recognize whether that sweetness came from God, from natural causes, or from delusion.

I began to seek the place of my heart in the manner Simeon the New Theologian taught. With my eyes closed I looked upon it in thought, i.e., in imagination. I tried to see it as it is in the left side of my breast and to listen attentively to its beating. At first I did it several times a day for half an hour, and failed to see anything but darkness. Then I succeeded in picturing my heart and the movement in it, and I learned how to bring in and out of it the Jesus Prayer, timing it with my breathing. In this I followed the teaching of Saint Gregory of Sinai, Saint Callistus, and Saint Ignatius. While inhaling, I saw my heart in my mind and said: "Lord Jesus Christ." In breathing out, I said: "Have mercy on me." This I did for an hour at a time, later for two hours, then as long as I was able to. Finally, I succeeded in doing it almost all day long. If things were hard to manage and I fell prey to laziness and doubt, I hastened to open the *Philocalia* and to read passages dealing with the action of the heart, and then once more I felt a fervent and eager desire for the prayer.

About three weeks later I noticed that my heart ached. Afterward this pain was transformed to the delightful sensation of warmth, comfort and peace. This incited me still further and urged me to the saying of the prayer with greater care. My thoughts dwelt constantly on it and I felt a great joy. From that time on I began to experience occasionally a great many different sensations in my heart and my mind. Now and then my heart would brim over with happiness overwhelmed by such lightness, freedom and solace that I was all changed and enraptured. At times I felt a glowing love for Jesus Christ and all God's creatures; and my eyes filled with tears of gratitude to God, Who poured His grace on me, a great sinner. As for my mind, so dull before, it sometimes received such an enlightenment that I was able to understand easily and to meditate upon things that hitherto had been beyond my comprehension. Now and then a sensation of delightful warmth would spread from my heart throughout my whole being, and I would be profoundly moved in recognizing God's presence in all things. Again, when I called upon the Name of Jesus I would be overwhelmed with bliss, and the meaning of "The Kingdom of Heaven is within you" would become clear to me.

From these and other, similar, comforting experiences I drew the conclusion that the results of inner prayer are threefold: it manifests itself in the spirit, in feelings and in revelations; the *spirit* is filled by a mellowness that comes from the love of God, inward calmness, exultation of mind, purity of thoughts and sweet remembrance of God. The *feelings* convey to us a delightful warmth of the heart, a joyful exultation, lightness and vigor, enjoyment of life and insensibility to pain and sorrow. The *revelation* brings us enlightenment of the mind, understanding of the Holy Scriptures and of the speech of all creatures, freedom from vanities, awareness of the sweetness of the inner life and cognizance of the nearness of God and of His love for mankind.

After having spent some five months in solitude and prayer, which filled me with sweet sensations, I grew so used to it that I practiced it constantly. In the end I felt that it was going on by itself in my mind and heart, not only while I was awake but also in my sleep. It never ceased for a single moment in whatever business I might have been doing. My soul gave thanks to God, and my heart melted away in continuous joy.

The time came for the felling of the trees. People began to arrive in great numbers, and I was compelled to leave my silent abode. I thanked the forester, prayed, kissed the plot of land on which God had showed his grace to me, unworthy of His mercy, donned my knapsack and set off. I wandered for a long time in different places until I reached Irkutsk. The self-acting Prayer of the Heart comforted and braced me on my journey. Wherever I found myself, whatever I did, it was never in my way, nor was it hindered by anything at all. When I was working at something with the inner Prayer of the Heart, my business progressed more readily. Whether I was listening to something attentively or reading, the prayer still went on at the same time. I was cognizant of both things simultaneously, as though my personality had been split and there were two souls in my body. Almighty God! How mysterious is the nature of man. "How manifold are Thy works, O Lord! In wisdom hast Thou made them all."

On my way I met with many adventures and happenings. If I were to relate them I should not finish in twenty-four hours. Here is an example of it! One winter evening I was walking alone through the woods toward a village about two versts away, where I was to take a night's rest, when a big wolf sprang at me all of a sudden. I held in my hand the wooden rosary of my elder, which I always carried with me, and made the motion of striking the animal with it. The rosary somehow or other encircled the neck of the wolf and was pulled out of my hand. As he leapt away from me, the wolf caught his hind paws in a thorny bush. Furiously he dashed about but failed to extricate himself, for the rosary, also caught on the branch of a dead tree, was tightening around his neck. I crossed myself in faith and went to set him free, mainly because I feared that if the rosary snapped, he might run off with my precious possession. And sure enough, scarcely had I got hold of the rosary when he broke free and darted away, leaving not a trace. I gave thanks to God and thinking of the elder on my way, I came hale and hearty to the village inn, where I asked for shelter.

At the comer table in the inn two men sat drinking tea. One of them was old, the other middle-aged and stout. They did not look like ordinary folk, and I asked the peasant caring for their horses who they were. He said that the old man was a teacher in the elementary school, and the other a clerk in the district court. Both belonged to the gentry. The peasant was taking them to the fair some twenty versts away.

After sitting there for a while I borrowed a needle and thread from a woman, drew closer to the candlelight and began to mend my broken rosary.

The clerk noticed it and said: "You've been praying so hard that you broke your rosary?"

"It was not I who broke it, it was the wolf," I answered.

"What! A wolf? Say, do wolves pray too?" he said humorously.

I told them the whole story and explained why the rosary was so dear to me. The clerk laughed: "To you bigots," he said, "miracles seem always to happen. What is miraculous about all this? The wolf was frightened and ran off simply because you hurled something at him. It is a known fact that wolves and dogs are scared by the gesture of hurling, and getting caught in the thicket is also quite common. Many things happen in the world. Shall we see miracles everywhere?"

Hearing this the schoolteacher shook his head: "Don't say that, sir," he replied, "you are not expert in science. As for me, I can readily see in this peasant's story the mystery of nature, which is sensuous and spiritual at the same time."

"How is that?" asked the clerk.

"It is like this. Though you have not received any higher education, you are nevertheless familiar with the sacred history of the Old and New Testaments through the catechetical instructions we use in our schools. Do you remember that when Adam, the first man, still enjoyed the state of holy innocence all animals were obedient to him, approached him in reverence and received their names from him? The elder who owned this rosary was a saint. And what is sanctity? It is the return of the sinner to the innocence of the first man. When the soul is holy, the body too becomes sanctified. This rosary had always been in the possession of a saintly man. Thus the touch of his hands and the emanations of his body had endowed it with the holy power of the first man's innocence. This is a mystery of spiritual nature. Now then: all animals in succession, down to our own times, have experienced this power naturally by means of the sense of smell, for in all animals the nose is the main organ of the senses. This is the mystery of sensuous nature."[5]

"You learned men are always talking about forces and wisdoms. For my part, I take things more simply. Fill your tumbler with vodka and send it down, and you'll have all the force you want," said the clerk, and he went to the cupboard.

"That is your business. As for the learned matters, pray, leave them to us," said the schoolteacher.

I liked the way he talked, so I approached him and said: "May I tell you, sir, a few more things about my elder?"

And I told him how the elder appeared to me in my dream, how he had instructed me, and made the charcoal mark in the *Philocalia*. The schoolteacher listened attentively, but the clerk, who had stretched out on the bench, grumbled: "It is true enough when they say that people go out of their mind from reading the Bible too often. That is what it is! What devil would come up at night to mark your book? You let it drop down yourself in your sleep and got it soiled with soot. There is your miracle. Ah, you cunning old fox! I have come across plenty of your kind!"

Mumbling this, he rolled over to the wall and fell asleep.

At these words, I turned to the schoolteacher and said: "I'll show you, if I may, the very book, which was really marked and not just soiled with soot." I took the *Philocalia* from my knapsack and showed him. "What amazes me," I said, "is how a disembodied spirit could have picked up a piece of charcoal and written with it."

The schoolteacher looked at the mark and began to speak: "This, too, is a mystery of the spirit. I will explain it to you. You see, when spirits appear in a physical form to a living man, they compose for themselves a palpable body from the air and the particles of light. After their appearance, they return to the elements what they have taken out for the composition of their bodies. And since the air possesses elasticity—a capacity of contraction and expansion—the soul vested in it can take anything and act and write. But let me see your book." He took it and chanced to open at the sermon of Saint Simeon the New Theologian. "Ah," he said, "this must be a theological book. I have never seen it before."

"This book, sir, consists almost entirely of instructions on inner prayer in the Name of Jesus Christ. It is revealed here in full detail by twenty-five holy fathers," I told him.

"I also know something about inner prayer," said the schoolteacher.

I bowed before him to the ground and asked him to tell me what he knew of it.

"Well, the New Testament tells us that men and all creation 'are subject to vanity not willingly,' but sigh and long for the liberty of the children of God. This mysterious sighing of all creation, the innate longing of souls for God, is inner prayer. There is no need to learn it, for it is inherent in everything and everyone."

"But how is one to find it, to discover it in one's heart, to take it by one's own will that it may act manifestly, give gladness, light and salvation?" I asked.

"I don't remember whether there is anything concerning this subject in theological treatises," said the schoolteacher.

"Oh, yes, there is. Everything is explained here," I said, pointing at the book.

He took out a pencil, wrote down the title of the *Philocalia* and declared: "I shall most certainly have a copy sent me from Tobolsk, and examine it." After that we separated, and when I started off, I thanked God for this conversation with the schoolteacher. As for the clerk, I prayed that our Lord would cause him to read the *Philocalia,* be it only once, and let him find through it enlightenment and salvation.

Another time, in spring, I came to a village, and it so happened that I stayed in the house of a priest. He was a kindly man, living quite alone. I spent three days with him. When he had observed me for that length of time, he said: "Stay here; you will be paid. I am looking for a dependable man. We are building a new stone church near the old wooden chapel. I need a trustworthy person to keep an eye on the workmen and stay in the chapel to take care of the collection for the building fund. It is just the sort of thing you can do, and will suit your way of life perfectly. You will sit alone in the chapel and pray. There is a quiet little room for the watchman there. Do stay, please, at least until the church has been built."

I refused repeatedly, but finally I had to yield to the priest's urging, and I remained there until fall, taking up my abode in the chapel. In the beginning it seemed to be quiet and suitable for prayer, though a great number of people came to the chapel, particularly on holy days. Some of them came to say their prayers, others to fritter away time and still others with the hope of filching money from the collection plate.

Sometimes I read the Bible and the *Philocalia*; some of the visitors saw this and started a conversation; others asked me to read out loud for them.

After a while I noticed a young peasant girl who came frequently to the chapel and spent a long time in prayer. Giving ear to her mumbling, I discovered that some of the prayers were very strange and the others were completely distorted. I asked her where she had learned them; she said that it was from her mother, who belonged to the church. Her father, however, was connected with a sect that had no priesthood. I felt sorry for her and advised her to say the prayers correctly, according to the traditions of Holy Church. Then I taught her the right wording of the Lord's Prayer and of the Hail Mary, and finally told her: "Say the Prayer of Jesus as often as you can, for it reaches God sooner than any other and will lead you to the salvation of your soul."

The girl heeded my advice and followed it carefully. And what happened? A short while afterward, she told me that she had grown so accustomed to the Jesus Prayer that she felt an urge to say it all the time. She was filled with gladness and the desire to recite it over and over again. This made me very happy, and I advised her to go on with the prayer in the name of Jesus Christ.

Summer was ending. Many of the visitors to the chapel wished to see me, not only for the sake of the reading and advice, but also to tell me all their worldly troubles and even to find out about things they had lost or mislaid. It seemed as though some of them took me for a sorcerer. The girl I had already mentioned also came to me in a state of great distress to ask advice. Her father wanted her to marry, against her will, a man of his sect. The wedding was to be performed not by a priest, but by a simple peasant. "But this marriage cannot be lawful," cried the girl. "Is it not the same thing as fornication? I will run away some place."

"But where?" I asked. "They will find you anywhere. Nowadays you can hide nowhere without a passport. They'll find you! You had better pray to God fervently to change your father's mind and to safeguard your soul from heresy and sin. This is a much better plan than flight."

As time went on I began to feel that all this noise and confusion were more than I could endure. Finally, at the end of summer, I determined to leave the chapel and go on with my wanderings as before. I told the priest of my plans: "You know my condition, Father! I must have peace for my prayers. This place is disturbing and harmful to me. Now that I have shown you my obedience, and stayed here the whole summer, let me go with your blessings on my solitary journey."

The priest did not wish to let me go. He tried to change my mind: "What hinders you from praying here? Apart from staying in the chapel, your work amounts to nothing, and you have your daily bread. You may say your prayers day and night if you wish, but stay here and live with God, brother.

You are of great help to me. You do not go for foolish talk with visitors, you are scrupulous with the collection money, and are a source of profit to the House of God. This is worth more than your solitary prayer. Why do you wish to be always alone? Community prayers are pleasanter. God did not create men to live only to themselves, but to help each other and lead each other on the path of salvation. Think of the saints and the Church Fathers. Day and night they worked hard, cared for the needs of the Church and preached in many places. They didn't sit down in solitude, hiding themselves from people."

"God gives everyone a special gift, Father," I said. "There have been many preachers, but also many hermits. Each has done what he could in his own way and in faith that God Himself was showing him the path of salvation. How do you explain the fact that many of the saints gave up their work as bishops, priests or abbots and retired into the desert to get away from the confusion that comes from living with other people? Thus, Isaac the Syrian, who was a bishop, left his flock. The venerable Athanasius of Athos abandoned his large monastery; and just because their places became a source of temptation to them. For they firmly believed in our Lord's saying: 'What shall it profit a man if he gain the whole world and lose his own soul?'"

"To be sure," said the priest, "but they were saints!"

"If saints must guard themselves from the hazards of mingling with people, what else can a weak sinner do?" I answered.

In the end I bade farewell to the kindly priest, who sent me on my way with the love in his heart.

Some ten versts further on, I stopped in a village for the night. At the inn there was a peasant so gravely ill that I recommended that those who were with him should see that he received the last sacraments. They agreed with me, and toward the morning they sent for the parish priest. I remained, for I wished to worship and pray in the Presence of the Eucharist. While waiting for the priest, I went into the street and sat on the bench there. All of a sudden I saw running toward me from the backyard the girl who used to pray in the chapel.

"What are you doing here?" I asked.

"They have set the day for my betrothal to the sectarian, so I ran away." Then she knelt before me and said: "Have pity on me. Take me along with you and put me in a convent. I do not wish to marry. I wish to live in a convent and recite the Prayer of Jesus. They will listen to you and receive me."

"Look here," I said. "Where do you want me to take you? I don't know a single convent in the vicinity. Without a passport, I can't take you anywhere! No one would receive you. It would be quite impossible for you to hide at a time like this. They will get you at once. You would be sent home and punished as a tramp besides. You had better go home and pray. If you do not want to marry, pretend that you are ill. It is called a saving dissimulation. The holy mother Clementa did it, and so did Saint Marina, when she took refuge in a monastery of men, and many others."

While we sat there discussing the matter, we saw four peasants driving up the road with a pair of horses. They came straight to us at a gallop, seized the girl and placed her in the cart. One of them drove off with her. The other three tied my hands together and forced me back to the village where I had passed my summer. In answer to all my objections they yelled: "We'll teach you, you fake saint, not to seduce girls."

In the evening I was brought up into the village court. My feet were put in irons and I was left in the prison to await my trial the next morning. The priest, upon learning that I was in jail, came to see me. He brought me some supper, consoled me and promised to intercede for me as a spiritual father by saying that I was not the kind of man they believed me to be. He sat with me for a while and then left for home.

The district police officer came late in the evening. He was driving through the village on his way somewhere else and put up at the deputy's house. They told him what had happened, and a peasant meeting was called. I was brought again to the village court. We went in and stood there waiting. In came the officer in a tipsy swagger, sat on the table with his cap on and shouted: "Hey, Epiphan! Did the girl, that daughter of yours, swipe anything from your house?"

"No, sir!"

"Has she been caught in doing anything wrong with that blockhead there?"

"No, sir!"

"Very well: this is what our judgment and decision will be. You manage your daughter yourself. As for this fellow, we'll give him a good lesson tomorrow and banish him from the village with strict orders never to return again. That is all."

So saying, the officer got down from the table and went off to bed, while I was put back in prison. Early in the morning two village policemen came, whipped me, and let me go.

I went my way thanking God for having esteemed me worthy to suffer in His Name. This thought consoled me and infused a new glow into my incessant prayer. None of these incidents touched me very deeply. It was as if I had seen them happen to somebody else, being myself a mere spectator of it all. Even when I was whipped, I had the power to bear it; the prayer that gladdened my heart made me unaware of anything else.

When I had gone about four versts, I met the girl's mother, who was driving from the market with her purchases. She saw me and said that the bridegroom had turned her daughter down. "You see," she added, "he was angry with Akulka for having fled from him." Thereupon, she gave me bread and a pie and I went on.

A long time after this another thing happened. I may tell you about it too. It was the 24th of March—I felt an irresistible desire to make my Communion the following morning, which was the Feast of the Annunciation of our Lady. I asked for the nearest church and was told that there was one some thirty versts away. So I walked the rest of that day and the whole night in order to arrive in time for Matins. The weather was very bad; a cold wind blew strongly; it was snowing and raining in turn. On my way I had to cross a brook; just as I got to the middle, the ice broke under my feet and I fell into the water up to my waist. Drenched as I was, I came to Matins, stood through it and through Mass, at which I made my Communion, by the grace of God. As I wished to spend a peaceful day in order to enjoy my spiritual happiness, I asked the warden permission to stay in his guardroom until the following morning. My heart was filled with indescribable happiness and joy. I lay there on the planks in the unheated room, as happy as if I were resting on Abraham's bosom. And the prayer was surging in my heart. The love of Jesus Christ and His Blessed Mother swept over me in waves of sweetness and immersed my soul in rapture and delight. At nightfall, however, a sharp pain set in in my legs, and I remembered that they were wet. I paid no attention to it, but listened attentively to the prayer in my heart and was no longer conscious of the discomfort. But in the morning when I tried to get up, I found that I could not move my legs. They were paralyzed and weak as bits of straw. The warden dragged me down off the plank bed. Motionless, I sat in the guardhouse for two days. On the third day he began to drive me out saying: "Should you die here, think of the mess I would be in."

I crawled out on my arms with great difficulty and made for the church. There I lay on the steps for another couple of days. The people who passed by paid no attention to me or my pleading. Finally, a peasant came up, sat beside me and talked. After a while he asked, casually: "What will you give me if I cure you? I used to suffer from exactly the same thing, and I know a drug for it."

"I have nothing to give you," I answered.

"What do you have in your bag?"

"Just some rusk and books."

"Well, maybe you'll work for me at least one summer if I cure you?"

"I can't do that either. See, I can use only one arm, the other is almost completely withered."

"What can you do then?"

"Nothing much, except read and write."

"Ah, you can write! Well then, teach my little boy to write. He can read a little, and I wish him to know how to write. But the masters are dear. They ask twenty rubles to teach him."

I consented to do it. With the help of the warden, he dragged me to his backyard and installed me in an old and empty bathhouse there. Then he began to treat me. He picked from the fields, yards and cesspools all sorts of putrid bones of cattle and birds, washed them carefully, broke them up with a stone and put them in a large earthen vessel. This he covered with a lid having a small perforation in it and placed upside down on an empty jar sunk in the ground. He covered the upper vessel with a thick layer of clay, and put a pile of wood around it, which he kept burning for twenty-four hours. "We'll extract some tar from these bones," he said, as he was feeding the fire. The following day, when he raised the jar from the ground, there was in it about a pint of thick, oily, reddish liquid, which dripped through the perforation in the lid of the upper vessel. This liquid had the strong smell of fresh raw meat. The bones in the earthen vessel were no longer black and decayed, but looked white, clean and transparent, like mother of pearl. With this liquid, I rubbed my legs five times a day. And what happened? In twenty-four hours I was able to move my toes. On the third day I could bend and unbend my legs. On the fifth day I stood on my feet and walked through the yard, leaning on a stick. In a word, within a week my legs had become as strong as they were before. I gave thanks to God, musing upon His wisdom and the mysterious power hidden in all creation. Dry, decayed bones, almost completely disintegrated, keep in themselves vital force, color and smell, and can act upon living bodies, communicating life to those that are already half-dead. This is a pledge of the future resurrection of the flesh. I wished that I could point this out to the forester with whom I had lived, remembering how uncertain he had been about the resurrection.

Having in this manner recovered from my illness, I began to teach the lad. I wrote out the Jesus Prayer as a sample of calligraphy, and made him copy the words carefully. To teach him was a restful occupation, for during the day he worked for the bailiff of the estate nearby and came to me while the latter slept—that is, from dawn to late Mass. The youngster was bright and soon began to write fairly well. When the bailiff found that he could write, he asked who his teacher was.

"A one-armed pilgrim who lives in our old bathhouse," the boy told him. The bailiff, who was a Pole, took interest in me and came to look me up. He found me reading the *Philocalia,* and he started a conversation by asking: "What are you reading?" I showed him the book.

"Ah," he said, "the *Philocalia*! I saw it in the house of our priest[6] when I lived in Vilno. I was told, however, that it contains all sorts of tricks and artifices for prayer laid down by Greek monks. It is like those fanatics of India and Bokhara who sit and inflate themselves trying to get a ticklish sensation in their hearts and in their foolishness take this purely physical reaction for prayer, considering it to be the gift of God. One must pray simply so as to fulfill our duty to God, stand and recite Our Father as Christ taught us. That will put you in the right groove for the whole day, but not the repetition of the same thing over and over again. That, I dare say, might drive you mad and injure your heart besides."

"Don't speak that way about this holy book, my dear sir!" I said. "It was not written by simple Greek monks, but by great and holy men of ancient times, by men revered by your own church, such as Anthony the Great, Macarius the Great, Mark the Hermit, John Chrysostom and others. The 'heart method' of inner prayer was taken over from them by the monks of India and Bokhara, who spoiled and distorted it, as my elder told me. In the *Philocalia,* however, all the instructions concerning the action of the prayer in the heart have been taken from the Word of God, from the Holy Bible in which the same Jesus Christ who commanded us to recite the Our Father taught also the incessant Prayer of the Heart. He said: '*Thou shalt love the Lord thy God with all thy heart and with all thy mind*'; '*Watch and pray*'; '*Abide in Me and I in you.*' And the holy Fathers, referring to the holy words of the Psalms, '*O taste, and see that the Lord is sweet,*' explain this passage in the following way: 'A Christian must seek and find, by every possible means, delight in prayer. He must look constantly for consolation in it and not be satisfied by merely saying "Our Father" once a day.' Now let me read to you how they censure those who do not try to find the happiness of the Prayer of the Heart. The wrong of such is threefold: (1) because they contradict the Scripture inspired by God; (2) because they do not strive for the higher and more perfect state of the soul, but are satisfied with outward virtues, and neither hunger nor thirst for truth, thus depriving themselves of blessedness and joy in the Lord; (3) because, in constantly thinking of themselves and their outward virtues, they often lapse into temptation or pride and thus fall into danger."

"What you are reading is too lofty," said the bailiff; "for us worldly people, it is hard to grasp."

"Well, let me read you something easier about men of goodwill, who, though they lived in the world, had learned how to pray incessantly." I found in the *Philocalia* the sermon by Simeon the New Theologian on the youth George and read it to him.

The bailiff was very pleased and said: "Lend me this book for a while. I will read it some day at my leisure."

"I may give it to you for twenty-four hours, but not for longer," I answered, "for I read it every day myself and can't live without it."

"Well, then, at least copy out for me what you have just read. I'll pay you."

"I don't want you to pay me. I will make a copy for you in brotherly love, and in hope that God will grant you a desire for prayer."

It was with pleasure that I copied for him the sermon at once. He read it to his wife and they both liked it. Thus it came to pass that they would send for me now and then, and I would take the *Philocalia* and read to them while they sat drinking tea and listening. One day they kept me for dinner. The bailiff's wife, a kindly old lady, sat with us at the table and ate fried fish. By some mishap, she swallowed a bone, which got stuck in her throat, and all our efforts to relieve her failed. She suffered a great ache, and in an hour or so was compelled to lie down. They sent for a doctor who lived thirty versts away. In the evening, feeling very sorry for her, I went home.

While I was sleeping lightly that night, I heard the voice of my elder. I did not see him but heard him speak to me. "Your landlord cured you; why, then, don't you try to cure the bailiff's wife? God has bidden us to feel pity for our neighbors."

"I would have helped her gladly, but how? I do not know!" I answered.

"Well, what you must do is this: from her early youth she had an aversion for olive oil, not only when she tastes it, but even its smell makes her very ill. Let her drink a spoonful of it. She will be nauseated, the bone will come out, but the oil will have a soothing effect on the sore in her throat and she will recover."

"And how am I to give it to her since she dislikes it so? She won't swallow it."

"Let the bailiff hold her head and pour it in her mouth even though you have to use force."

I woke up, rushed to the bailiff and told him all this in detail.

"Of what use can your oil be now? She is wheezing and delirious, and her neck is swollen. However, we may try, even if it doesn't help. Oil is a harmless medicine."

He poured some into a wine glass and we made her swallow it. Seized with nausea at once, she ejected the bone along with some blood and was greatly relieved. Soon she fell into a profound sleep. In the morning I came to inquire about her health and found her sitting peacefully at the tea table. She marveled with her husband at the way she had been cured. But what surprised them even more was the fact that her dislike of oil that had been told me in a dream was not known to anyone except to themselves. At that time the doctor drove up and the bailiff's wife told him of her experience. For my part, I told him how the peasant had cured my legs. The doctor heard us through and said: "I am not surprised at either of the cases, for the forces of nature operated in both of them. However, I shall take note of it." And he wrote with the pencil in his notebook.

After this the rumor quickly spread throughout the neighborhood that I was a seer, a doctor and a healer. People streamed to me from all parts to consult with me on their affairs and their troubles. They brought me presents, treated me with reverence and pampered me. I endured all this a week. Then, fearing that I might succumb to the temptation of vainglory, I left the place in secrecy at night.

Once more I started on my lonely journey, feeling as light as if a heavy load had been lifted off my shoulders. The prayer comforted me more than ever, and at times my heart was glowing with boundless love for Jesus Christ. This joyous bubbling seemed to send flows of consolation through my whole body. The mental representation of Jesus Christ was so vivid that when I meditated on the events related in the Gospel, I seemed to see them before my very eyes. Moved to tears of joy, I sometimes felt such happiness in my heart as I have no words to describe.

It happened at times that for three days or more I came upon no human habitations, and in the exaltation of my spirit I felt as though I were all alone on this earth, just one miserable sinner before the merciful and man-loving God. This sense of complete solitude comforted me, and the rapture I experienced in my prayers was much stronger than when I was among many people.

At last I reached Irkutsk. When I had made my prostrations and said my prayers before the relics of Saint Innocent, I began to wonder: "Where shall I go now?" I did not care to stay there for a long time, for it was a large and crowded city. I was going along the streets, deep in my thoughts, when a local merchant stopped me and asked: "You are a pilgrim, aren't you? Won't you come to my house?" He took me to his wealthy home and asked me where I came from. I told him all about my beginnings. He listened and said:

"You should go to Jerusalem on a pilgrimage. That place is more sacred than any other site on earth."

"I should be only too happy to do so," I said, "but I haven't the means of going there. I could get along until I reached the sea, but I cannot afford the voyage. It costs a great deal."

"If you wish me to, I can get the money for you. Last year I sent an old man there, one of our townspeople," said the merchant.

I sank to his feet in gratitude. "Listen," he continued, "I'll give you a letter to my son who lives in Odessa. He has business connections with Constantinople and sends his own ships; he will be pleased to arrange your transportation on one of his boats there. One of his agents will book a passage from Constantinople to Jerusalem for you. He will pay; it does not cost much."

When I heard this I was overcome with happiness and thanked my benefactor for his kindness. Even more did I thank God for the fatherly love and care He showed to me, a wretched sinner, who did no good either to himself or to men, but ate in idleness the bread belonging to others.

I stayed with the generous merchant for three days. He wrote me a letter to his son as he had promised. And now, here I am on my way to Odessa with the intention of reaching the Holy City of Jerusalem. Yet, I do not know whether the Lord will permit me to pray in reverence at His life-giving tomb.

Part Three

JUST BEFORE LEAVING Irkutsk I called on my spiritual father with whom I had had so many talks, and said to him: "Now that I am ready to go to Jerusalem, I have come to take leave of you and to thank you for your love for me in Christ, unworthy wanderer that I am."

"May God bless your journey," answered the priest. "But tell me about yourself—who you are and where do you come from? About your travels I have already heard a great deal. Now, I should like to know more about your life before you became a pilgrim."

"Well, I'll gladly tell you about that also. It is not a long story," I answered.

I was born in a village in the province of Orel. After our parents died, there were just the two of us left, my elder brother and I. He was ten years old and I was two. We were adopted by my grandfather, an honorable man, quite well-off. He kept an inn on the main road, and because of his kindness many people stayed in his place. My brother, who was a high-spirited boy, spent most of his time in the village. I preferred to stay near my grandfather. On Sundays and holy days we would go to church together, and at home my grandfather would read the Bible—this very Bible I carry with me now. My brother grew up and turned bad. He began to drink.

Once, when I was seven years old and we were both lying in bed, he pushed me down; I fell and injured my left arm. Never since have I been able to use it; it's all withered up.

My grandfather, seeing that I should never be able to work in the fields, taught me to read from this Bible, for we had no spelling book. He pointed at the letters, made me learn them and form the words. I can hardly understand it myself, but somehow or other by repeating things over and over again, I learned to read after a while. Later, when his eyesight grew weak, he often bade me read to him, and corrected me as he listened. A certain village clerk often put up at our inn. He wrote a beautiful hand. I watched him write and liked it. Then I began to copy words at his direction. He gave me paper and ink and quill pens. Thus I learned to write. My grandfather was very pleased and admonished me: "God has given you the knowledge of reading and writing, which will make a man of you. Give thanks to the Lord and pray often."

We used to attend all the services at church, and at home said our prayers frequently. I was always made to read the fifty-first psalm, and while I did so, grandfather and grandmother knelt or made their prostrations.

My grandmother died when I was seventeen years old. After a while my grandfather told me: "There is no longer a mistress in this house, and that is not right. Your brother is good for nothing, and I am going to look for a wife for you." I refused, saying that I was a cripple, but my grandfather insisted, and I got married. My wife was a quiet and good girl about twenty years old. A year later my grandfather fell hopelessly ill. Feeling that death was near, he called me, bade me farewell, and said:

"My house and all I have is yours. Live according to your conscience; deceive no one, and above all, pray, for everything comes from God. Trust in Him only. Go to church regularly, read your Bible and remember your grandmother and me in your prayers. Here, take this money. There are a thousand rubles here; be thrifty, do not waste it, but don't be stingy either; give to the poor and to God's church." Soon after this he died and I buried him.

My brother begrudged me the property, which was left entirely to me. He grew more and more angry, and the Enemy incited him against me to such an extent that he even planned to do away with me. Finally, this is what he did one night while we slept and no guests stayed in the inn. He broke into the storeroom where the money was kept, took it from the chest and set fire to the storeroom. The flames spread rapidly through the whole house before we were aware of them, and we barely escaped with our lives by jumping from the window in our nightclothes. The Bible was lying under our pillow. We grabbed it, and took it with us. As we looked at our burning home, we said to one another: "Thank God, we saved the Bible. This, at least, is a comfort in our misfortune."

Thus, all we possessed burned to ashes, and my brother had disappeared without a trace. Later on we learned that while on a spree, he was heard to boast that he had stolen the money and set fire to the house.

We were left naked and barefoot, like beggars. With some money we borrowed, we built a little hut and set out to lead the life of landless peasants. My wife was a nimble-fingered person. She knew how to knit, spin and sew. People gave her work; she toiled day and night and supported me. For my part, I was not even able to make bast shoes. My crippled arm made me quite useless. And while my wife was knitting or spinning, I would sit next to her and read the Bible. She would listen to me, but sometimes she would begin to weep. When I asked her: "Why are you weeping? We are still alive, thank God!" she would answer: "It is that beautiful writing in the Bible. It moves me so deeply!"

Remembering my grandfather's bidding, we fasted often, said the *Acathistos*[7] to Our Lady every morning, and at night made a thousand prostrations to keep away from temptation. In this manner we lived for two years in peace. But this is what is really astonishing; although we had no idea of the inner, heart-acted prayer, but prayed with our lips only and made senseless prostrations, turning somersaults like fools, we nevertheless felt the desire for prayer, and the long ones we recited without understanding did not seem tiring; quite the contrary—we enjoyed them a great deal. It must be true, as a certain teacher once told me, that secret prayer is hidden deeply in the heart of man, though he may not know about it. Yet, it acts mysteriously within his soul and prompts him to pray according to his power and knowledge.

After two years of that kind of life, my wife suddenly fell ill with a high fever. She received Communion and passed away on the ninth day of her illness. Now I was left completely alone. Unable to work, I was compelled to beg, though I was ashamed of it. Besides, I was grief-stricken at the loss of my wife and did not know what to do with myself. If I happened to enter our hut and see her dress, or maybe a kerchief, I would cry out or even faint away. Life at home was beyond my endurance. Therefore I sold my hut for twenty rubles and gave to the poor whatever clothes my wife and I had possessed. Because of my withered arm, I was given a passport that exempted me for good from public duties. And taking my beloved Bible I left, neither caring nor even knowing where I was going. But after I had set off I began to wonder where I should go. "First of all," I said to myself, "I will go to Kiev. There I will pray at the shrines of saints and ask for relief in my sorrow." As soon as my decision was made, I began to feel better, and reached Kiev greatly comforted. Since then, for the last thirteen years I have been going from place to place. I have visited many churches and monasteries, but now I prefer to wander in the steppes and the fields. I don't know whether God will let me go to Jerusalem. There, if it is His Divine will, it is high time for my sinful bones to be laid to rest.

"And how old are you now?"

"I am thirty-three years of age."

"The age of our Lord Jesus Christ."

Part Four

"TELL ME MORE about the edifying experiences you have encountered in your wanderings," said my spiritual Father. "It was with great pleasure and interest that I listened to what you told me before."

"I shall do it gladly," I answered, "for I have lived through many things, good and bad. But it would take a long time to tell of them all; besides, I have already forgotten a great deal; I have always tried to remember only that which guided and urged my indolent soul to prayer. All the rest I remember but rarely. Or rather, I try to forget the past, as the Apostle Paul bids us. My late elder of blessed memory also used to say that forces opposed to the prayer in the heart assail us from two sides, from the right hand and the left. In other words, if the enemy cannot distract us from prayer by means of vain and sinful thoughts, he brings back edifying reminiscences into our minds, or fills them with beautiful ideas so that he may draw us away from the prayer—a thing that he cannot bear. This is called 'a theft from the right side,' where the soul, forgetting its intercourse with God, revels in a colloquy with itself or with other created things. Therefore, he taught me to shut myself off from even the most sublime spiritual thoughts whenever I am at prayer. And if at the end of the day I remembered that more time had been given to lofty ideas and talks than to the essential secret Prayer of the Heart, I was to consider it a sign of spiritual covetousness and immoderation.

"Yet, one cannot forget everything. An impression may have engraved itself so profoundly in one's memory that although it seems to be gone, it comes back in all its clarity even after a long while. Such are, for example, the few days God deemed me worthy to stay with a certain pious family:

One day as I was wandering through the province of Tobolsk, I found myself in a certain district town. My provision of rusk had run low, so I went to one of the houses to ask for some bread for my journey. The owner of the house told me: "Thank God you have come at the right time. My wife has just taken the bread out of the oven. Here you are, take this warm loaf. Remember us in your prayers." I thanked him and was putting the bread into my knapsack when his wife saw it and said: "Your knapsack is pretty wornout. I'll give you another instead," and she gave me a new and a stout one. I thanked them again from the bottom of my heart and went away. Before leaving the town I asked in a little shop for a bit of salt, and the shopkeeper gave me a small bag of it. I rejoiced in spirit and thanked God for letting me, unworthy as I was, meet such kind people. "Now," I thought, "I have not to worry about food for a whole week and shall sleep in peace. 'Bless the Lord, O my soul!'"

About five versts or so from that town, I passed through a poor village where I saw a little wooden church with lovely paintings and ornaments on its facade. I wished to honor the house of God and went up to the porch to pray. On the lawn beside the church, two little children, five or six years old, were playing. They might have been the parish priest's children, except that they were too well-dressed for that. After I had said my prayer, I went away. Scarcely had I gone a dozen steps when I heard them shout: "Dear beggar, dear beggar, stop!" The two mites I had just seen, a boy and a girl, were running after me. I stopped. They came up to me and took me by the hand. "Come with us to Mummy; she likes beggars," they said. "She will give you money for your journey."

"Where is your mummy?" I asked

"Over there, behind the church, behind that little grove."

They led me to a beautiful garden in the midst of which stood a large manor house. We went inside. How clean it was, and so beautifully furnished! In ran the lady of the house to greet me. "Welcome, welcome! God sent you to us. Where are you from? Sit down, sit down, dear." She took off my knapsack with her own hands, laid it on the table, and made me sit in a very soft chair. "Wouldn't you like something to eat, or perhaps some tea? Is there anything I can do for you?"

"I thank you most humbly," I answered, "but my bag is filled with food. As for tea, I do take it occasionally, but in our peasant way I am not used to it. But I shall pray that God may bless you for your kindness to strangers in the true spirit of the Gospel." As I said this I felt a strong urge to retire within myself. Prayer was bubbling in my heart and I needed peace and silence to give an outlet to its rising flame. I also wished to hide from others my sighs and tears, and the movements of my face and lips—these outward signs that follow prayer. Therefore I got up and said: "Excuse me, Lady, but I must go now. May the Lord Jesus Christ be with you and your dear little children."

"Oh, no! God forbid that you should go now. I won't let you. My husband will be back in the evening. He is a magistrate in the district court. How delighted he will be to see you."

So I stayed to wait for her husband, and gave her a short account of my journey.

Dinnertime came and we sat down to table. Four other ladies came in, and we began our meal. When we had finished the first course, one of them got up, bowed to the icon and then to us. Then she went out; she returned with the second course and sat down again. Then another of the ladies in the same manner fetched the third course. Seeing this I asked: "May I venture to ask if these ladies are related to you?"

"Yes, indeed! They are my sisters. This is my cook and this is the coachman's wife; that one is the housekeeper; the other is my maid. They are married, all of them. We have no unmarried girls in the house."

The more I heard and saw all this, the more I wondered and thanked God for having brought me to these pious people. The prayer was working strongly in my heart, and I wished to be alone, so as not to hinder its action. As we rose from the table, I said to the lady: "Surely you will want to rest after dinner, and I am so used to walking that I shall go to the garden for a while."

"I don't need a rest," said the lady. "Tell me something edifying, I will go to the garden with you. If you go alone the children will give you no peace. The moment they see you, they will not leave you at all. They have such a liking for beggars, brothers of Christ and pilgrims."

There was nothing I could do but go with her. We entered the garden. In order to remain silent myself, I bowed down to the ground before her and said: "Pray, tell me in the name of our Lord if you have lived that pious life very long. How did you come to it?"

"I will tell you the whole story," she answered: "My mother was a great-granddaughter of the bishop Joasaph, whose relics you may see in Belgorod. When she gave my husband and myself her motherly blessing, she bade us live as good Christians, to pray fervently but above all to carry out the greatest of all God's commandments, which is to love our neighbors, to feed and help beggarly brothers of Christ in humble simplicity, to bring up our children in the fear of God, and to treat the serfs as our own brothers. That is how we have been living here in retirement for the past ten years, trying to fulfill my mother's last wishes. We have a guesthouse for beggars. A few sick and crippled people are living there now. We may visit them tomorrow."

After we had gone indoors, her husband arrived. When he saw me, he greeted me with kindness. We kissed each other in a Christian and brotherly fashion. Then he led me to his own room, saying: "Come to my study, dear brother; bless my cell." We entered his study. How many books there were! and beautiful icons, too, and the life-giving Cross in full size, with a copy of the Gospels lying nearby. I said my prayer and turned to my host: "This is God' s paradise here!" Then I asked what kind of books he had.

"I have a great many religious books," he replied. "Here are the lives of the Saints for the whole year, the works of Saint John Chrysostom, Basil the Great and of many other theologians and philosophers. I also have many volumes of sermons by famous contemporary preachers. My library cost me five thousand rubles or so."

"Do you have anything on prayer?" I asked.

"Yes," he said, "I like very much to read about prayer. This is the very latest book on that subject written by a priest of Saint Petersburg." He took out the book on the Lord's Prayer, and we began to read it with interest. After a while the lady came in and brought us tea, and the little ones dragged a silver basket full of cakes such as I have never eaten before in my life. The gentleman took the book from me and handed it to his wife, saying: "Now, we'll make her read, she does it very well. And we shall have tea meanwhile." The lady began reading and we listened. As I did so the prayer became active in my heart, and I listened to it. The longer she read, the more intense became my prayer, and it filled me with joy. Suddenly I saw something flickering quickly before my eyes in the air, and I thought that it was my late elder. I gave a start, but tried to hide it and said by way of apology: "Pardon me, I must have dozed off for a moment." Then I felt as if the soul of my elder had penetrated into my own or was giving light to it. There was a sort of light in my mind and a great many thoughts concerning the prayer came to me in a flash. I crossed myself, trying to drive them away with my will as the lady finished the book and her husband asked me whether I liked it. We began to talk again.

"I liked it very much," I answered, "and 'Our Father' is the most sublime and the most precious of all the written prayers we Christians have, since it was given to us by our Lord Jesus Christ Himself. And the interpretation of the prayer that has just been read is a very good one, but it emphasizes mainly the active phase of Christian life, whereas in my reading of the Holy Fathers I have noticed a stress upon the speculative and mysterious side of it."

"In which of the Holy Fathers' works did you read this?"

"Well, for example, in the works of Maxim the Confessor and of Peter the Damascene as given in the *Philocalia*."

"Can you recall what they say? Do tell us."

"Why, certainly! The very first words of the prayer—'Our Father who art in Heaven' are interpreted in your book as an appeal to the brotherly love we must feel for each other since we all are children of the same Father—and this is quite true. The Holy Fathers, however, give to them another explanation that is more spiritual and profound. They say that we should lift our mind upwards to the Heavenly Father and remember every moment that we find ourselves in the presence of God.

"'The words 'Hallowed be Thy Name' are explained in your book in the following manner: we must be careful not to utter the Name of God without reverence, nor use it in false oaths; the Holy Name of God ought to be spoken in devotion but never in vain. Yet the mystical interpreters see here a direct call to inner prayer, so that the Most Holy Name of God may be engraved in the heart and hallowed by the self-acting prayer, and at the same time hallow all the feelings and powers of the soul. The words 'Thy Kingdom come' they interpret as a call to inward serenity, peace and spiritual contentment. Further, your book says that the words: 'give us our daily bread' must be understood as a request for the needs of our physical life, not in superfluousness, of course, but just that which we need for ourselves and for the help of our neighbors. But Maxim the Confessor understands by 'daily bread' the nourishment of the soul with the heavenly bread, which is the Word of God and the union of the soul with God by meditation upon Him and praying to Him incessantly in the heart."

"Ah! This is a great thing. But for lay people the attainment of inner prayer is well-nigh impossible," exclaimed the gentleman. "We may deem ourselves fortunate if God helps us to say our ordinary prayers without laziness."

"Don't think that, father. If it were impossible, or too difficult, God would not have bidden us all to do it. His strength manifests itself in weakness. And the Holy Fathers, rich in experience, show us easier ways to attain to inner prayer. Naturally, to the hermit they point out special and higher methods of procedure. But lay people also find in their writings convenient means that truly lead them to inner prayer."

"I have never read anything about the matter," he said.

"Well, if you wish to hear it, I will read to you from the *Philocalia*," I said, taking out my book. I found in part three, page 48, the treatise of Peter the Damascene and began to read: "One must call upon the Name of God even more often than one takes a breath, at all times, in all places in any kind of work. The Apostle says: 'Pray incessantly,' that is, he teaches men to remember God always, everywhere and in all situations. Whatever you do, keep in your mind the Maker of all things. When you behold light, remember who gives it to you; when you see heaven and earth and sea and all that they contain, be in awe and give praise to their Creator. When you put on your clothes, remember whose gift they are and give thanks to Him who takes care of your needs. In a word, remember and praise God in all your actions, and then you will be praying incessantly and your soul will be filled with gladness."

"Now, you see yourself how simple and easy the way of incessant prayer is," I said. "It is within the reach of everyone who still retains some sort of human feelings."[8]

They were greatly pleased with this. My host embraced me and thanked me again and again. In a while we went to supper and the whole household of men and women sat down to table as before. How reverently quiet and silent they were during the meal! After we finished, all of us, including the children, prayed for a long time. They had me read the *Acathistos* to Jesus the Most Lovable. Thereafter, the servants retired and the three of us remained alone. The lady went out of the room for a while and then came back with a pair of stockings and a white shirt, which she gave me. I bowed down to the ground before her and said: "I won't take stockings, my dear Lady; we peasants are used to leg bands." She left again and this time brought one of her old dresses of thin, yellow material and cut it into two leg bands. Her husband observed: "O, my poor man! his footwear is almost falling apart." In his turn he brought me his large, new overshoes, which are worn over the boots. "Go to the next room," he said, "there is nobody there, and you can change your shirt." I did so, and when I returned they made me sit down on a chair to put on my new footwear. He wrapped my feet and legs in the leg bands, and she put on the shoes. At first I would not let them, but they said: "Sit still and don't protest. Christ washed the feet of His disciples." There was nothing I could do but obey, and I began to weep. And they were weeping too. After this the lady retired for the night to the children's apartment and her husband took me to the summerhouse in the garden. There we had a long talk, after which we slept for an hour or so till we heard the Matins bells. We got ready and made our way to the church. The lady of the house and her little children had already been there for some time. We heard Matins; Mass began soon afterward. I could not help weeping when I saw the light on the faces of my host and his family as they prayed and knelt in devotion.

After the service the masters, the priest, the servants and all the beggars went to the dining room together. There were about forty beggars, some of them crippled and sickly looking. Among them were children too. All of us sat down at the table, and the meal was silent and peaceful as usual. Summoning my courage, I whispered to my host: "In convents and monasteries they read lives of the saints during meals. This could be done here. You have a set of volumes of the lives of the saints for the whole year round."

My host nodded: "Yes, indeed!" and turning to his wife said: "Let's do that, Masha. It will be most edifying! I will begin to read at the next dinner, then it will be your turn, after you the Reverend Father's and then all the brothers who can read will come next."

The priest, who had already begun his meal, said: "I'd love to listen. As for reading, with all respect, I should prefer not to. At home I am so busy that I don't know which way to turn from worries and obligations of all kinds. With that host of children and animals I must attend to my day is filled up. There is no time for reading or preparing sermons; I long ago forgot what I learned in the seminary."

Upon hearing this I shuddered, but the lady who was sitting beside me patted me on the hand and said: "Father talks like that out of sheer humility. He always belittles himself, but he is a most kindly and saintly man. He has been a widower for the last twenty years, and now takes care of his grandchildren, besides holding services very often." At these words I remembered the saying of Nicetas Stethatus in the *Philocalia*: "He who attains true prayer and love has no discrimination between things and sees no difference between the righteous man and a sinner, but loves them all and condemns no one, as God makes the sun shine and the rain fall upon both the just and the unjust."

Silence fell again. Opposite me sat a beggar who lived in the guesthouse. He was quite blind and the host took care of him. He cut fish for him, handed him a spoon and poured his soup.

As I looked at the beggar closely, I noticed that his mouth was always open and his tongue was moving as though it were trembling. I wondered if he wasn't one of those who recite the prayer, and I went on observing him. At the end of dinner an old woman fell suddenly ill; it must have been a serious attack, for she groaned from pain. The masters of the house took her into their bedroom and laid her on the bed. The lady remained there to look after her, and while the priest went to get the Reserved Sacrament, our host ordered his carriage and dashed to town to fetch a physician.

I felt as if I were hungry for the prayer. The urge to pour out my soul was strong, yet I had had no privacy and peace for nearly forty-eight hours. There was in my heart something like a flood that was about to burst out and overflow all my limbs. My attempt to hold it back caused me a sharp, though delightful, pain in my heart—a pain that could be soothed and calmed only in prayer and silence. Now it became clear to me why those who truly practice self-acting inner prayer avoid men and flee into the solitude of unknown places. I understood also why the venerable Hesychius considers even the most spiritual and useful talk to be but idle chatter if it is too prolonged, just as Ephrem the Syrian says: "Good speech is silver, but silence is pure gold."

Musing upon the matter, I went to the guesthouse, where everybody was resting after dinner. I went up to the attic; there I calmed down, rested and prayed.

When the beggars got up, I found the blind man and led him to the kitchen garden; we sat down alone and began to talk. "Pray, tell me for the love of my soul," I said, "do you recite the Prayer of Jesus?"

"Yes, indeed! I have been saying it without ceasing for a long time."

"What do you feel when you do so?"

"Only this, that I cannot live without praying day or night."

"How did God reveal it to you? Tell me about it in detail, dear brother."

"You see, I am a craftsman here. I used to earn my living by tailoring. I journeyed to other provinces, going from village to village and making peasant clothes. It happened that I lived for a long time in one village in the home of a peasant for whose family I was working. On some feast day I noticed three books lying by the icons and asked, 'Who is it can read them?'—'No one,' I was told. 'These books belonged to our uncle, who was very proficient in reading.' I took out one of these books, opened it at random and read the following words, which I remember to this day: 'Incessant prayer is calling upon the Name of God at all times. Whether one is talking or sitting down, walking, working or eating, or whatever one may be doing, it is meet that one should call on the Name of God in all the places and at all times.' When I read this I thought how easy this would be for me, and I began to do it behind my sewing machine and liked it. People who lived with me noticed it and made fun of me: 'What are you whispering all the time?' they asked. 'Are you a witch-master trying to cast a spell over someone?' I stopped moving my lips so as to hide what I was doing and continued saying the prayer with the tongue only and grew so accustomed to it that my tongue says it by itself day and night. I went about my business for a long time and then all of a sudden I became completely blind. In my family almost everyone got 'dark water' in the eyes. Because of my poverty our people placed me in the almshouse at Tobolsk—the capital of our province. I am on my way there now, but our hosts have kept me here, for they want to give me a cart to Tobolsk."

"What was the title of the book you read? Wasn't it called the *Philocalia?*"

"Frankly I couldn't tell I did not look at the title page."

I brought my *Philocalia* and found in part four those very words of the Patriarch Callistus, which the blind man recited by heart, and read them to him.

"Why! these are exactly the same words," he exclaimed. "Go on with your reading, brother. Isn't it wonderful!"

When I came to the line that "one must pray with the heart," he asked me with surprise: "What does it mean? How can this be done?"

I told him that a complete instruction on the prayer of heart was given in the same book, called the *Philocalia*, and he urged me to read it to him .

"Well, this is what we ought to do," I said. "When are you planning to leave for Tobolsk?"

"Right away, if you wish me to."

"All right, then. I am starting on my way tomorrow. We'll go together; I will read you all the passages that deal with prayer of the heart, and I will tell you how to find your heart and enter it."

"But how about the cart?" he asked.

"Ah, what do you need the cart for? Tobolsk is not too far, a mere hundred and fifty versts. We'll walk by easy stages, all by ourselves, you and I, talking and reading about the prayer as we go." So, our plans were made.

In the evening our host himself came to call us to supper. After the meal, we told him, the blind man and myself, that we were starting on our journey together. We explained that we did not need a cart, for we wished to read the *Philocalia* with more leisure.

The next morning we took the road after thanking our hosts most warmly for their great kindness and love. Both of them came with us about a verst from their house, and then we parted, bidding farewell to each other.

We walked in a leisurely fashion, the blind man and I, doing from ten to fifteen versts a day. And the remainder of our time we spent in lonely spots reading the *Philocalia*. When we had finished the required passages, he begged me to show him the means by which the mind may find the heart, and the divine Name of Jesus may be brought into it so that we could pray sweetly with the heart.

"Well," I said, "when you fix your eyes upon your hand or your foot, can't you picture them as clearly as if you were seeing them, although you are blind?"

"Indeed, I can," he answered.

"Then try to imagine your heart in the same way; fix your eyes upon it as if they were looking through your breast; picture it as vividly as you can, and listen attentively to its beating. When you have grown used to it, begin to time the words of the prayer with the beats of your heart. Thus, say or think 'Lord' with the first beat, 'Jesus' with the second, 'Christ' with the third, 'have mercy' with the fourth and 'on me' with the fifth. Repeat it over and over again. This you can do easily, for you have already made the preparation and the beginning of the Prayer of the Heart. Later, you must learn how to bring in and out of your heart the whole Prayer of Jesus, timing it with your breathing, as the Fathers taught. While inhaling, say, or imagine that you are saying, 'Lord Jesus Christ', and, as you breathe out, 'have mercy on me.' Repeat it as often as you can; in a short while your heart will hurt you, but in a light and pleasant way: and the feeling of warmth will spread throughout your whole body. However, beware of imagination! Don't let yourself be lured by visions of any kind. Ward them off, for the Holy Fathers bid urgently that the inner prayer should remain free from visions, lest we fall into delusions."

My blind friend listened to all this carefully and started at once to do what I had told him. At nightfall, when we stopped for a rest, he devoted himself to this practice for a long time. In about five days he began to feel in his heart a delightful warmth as well as a joy beyond words and a longing for incessant prayer, which stirred up in him the love for Jesus Christ. At certain times he saw light, though he could not discern objects. At other times, it seemed to him, when he entered the region of his heart, as though the flame of a burning candle flared up brightly in his bosom, and rushing outwards through his throat, filled him with light. And in this light he could see distant events, as it happened on one occasion when we were going through the forest. He was silent, wholly absorbed in the prayer. "What a pity," he cried all of a sudden. "The church is on fire and the tower has just collapsed."

"Stop imagining things," I said to him. "This is a temptation to you—nothing but idle fancies that must be put aside. How can anyone see what is happening in the city? It is still twelve versts away." He obeyed and continued to pray in silence. When we came to the city toward evening, I actually saw there a few burned houses and the fallen belfry, which had been built on wooden piles. There were throngs of people marveling that it had not crushed any one when it fell. As I figured it out, the catastrophe had occurred at exactly the time when the blind man had told me about it.

He turned to me and said: "You told me that this vision of mine was an idle fancy, but now you see that it was not. How can I fail to love and to thank our Lord Jesus Christ who shows His grace even to sinners, the blind and the unlearned? And I thank you, too, for having taught me how to attain the inner activity of the heart."

"Surely, you must love Jesus Christ and thank Him for His mercy," I answered, "but guard yourself from believing that your visions are a direct revelation of grace. They may occur frequently in a perfectly natural order of things. For neither space nor matter can bind the human soul. It cannot only see in darkness, but also things that are a long way off, as well as those that are nearby. Only we fail to develop this spiritual power to its fullest extent. We suppress it within our crude bodies, or crush it beneath the confusion of our muddled thoughts and ideas. But when we begin to concentrate, when we retire within ourselves and become more sensitive and subtle in the mind, then the soul fulfills its purpose and unfolds its highest power. This process is a natural one. I have heard from my departed elder that even people who are not given to prayer, but who are endowed with that kind of power or acquire it in sickness, can see in the darkest room the light flowing from every object and can perceive things in that light. They can even see their own doubles and enter into the thoughts of other people. However, all that comes directly from the grace of God by the Prayer of the Heart is filled with such sweetness and delight that no tongue can describe it, nor can it be compared to anything in the material world. For anything sensual is inferior when compared with the sweet realization of the grace in the heart."

My blind companion listened attentively and became more humble than ever. The prayer grew stronger and stronger in his heart and filled him with an ineffable delight. With all my soul I rejoiced at all this, and zealously thanked God who judged me worthy to see such a blessed servant of His.

At last we reached Tobolsk. I took him to the almshouse and left him there, bidding him a loving farewell. Then, once more, I set off on my way.

For about a month I went along at leisure, thinking of the way in which pure lives spur us on to follow their examples. I read the *Philocalia* attentively and reexamined everything I had told the devout blind man. His eagerness fired me with zeal, gratitude and love for God, and the Prayer of the Heart filled me with such gladness that I could not imagine a happier person on earth. Often I wondered whether the bliss in the Kingdom of Heaven could be greater and fuller. Not only did I feel happy within my soul, but the outside world, too, appeared delightful to me. Everything I saw aroused in me love and thankfulness to God; people, trees, plants, animals were all my kind, for I saw in all of them the reflection of the Name of Jesus Christ. At times I felt as light as if I were bodiless and floating blissfully in the air. At other times, when

I retired within myself, I was able to see my internal organs, and marveled at the wisdom with which the human body is formed. Then again I felt a joy as if I had been made Tsar, and at such moments of rapture I wished that God would let me die soon, so that I might pour out my gratitude at His feet in the realm of the spirits . . .

"I was led to experience a great many other things," I said, looking at my spiritual father, "but I should need more than three days and nights to relate to you all that happened. Still, there is one more incident I might tell you about:

One bright summer day I noticed at the side of the road a churchyard—what is usually called a *pogost*—(that is, a cemetery) a church and clergy-houses. The bells were ringing and I went to Mass with the people who lived in the neighborhood. Some of them sat down on the ground before they reached the church. Seeing that I was hurrying along, they told me not to rush: "When the service begins, you'll have to stand about for ages. The Mass here takes a long time. Our priest is sickly and slow."

As a matter of fact, the service did last a very long time. The priest was still young but emaciated and pale; he celebrated slowly but with great devotion, and his sermon at the end of the Mass was simple and beautiful. He preached of the way of acquiring the love of God.

After the Mass he invited me to his house and had me stay for dinner. I said to him while we sat at the table: "How slowly and reverently you celebrate, Father!"

"Yes, though my parishioners do not seem to like it," he answered. "They grumble, but I can't help it. For I believe that words uttered without inward feeling and attention are useless to myself as well as to others. What really matters is the inner life and intense prayer. But only few are concerned with the inner life. The reason is that they do not care about inward enlightenment."

"And how can one attain it?" I asked. "Is it not very difficult?"

"Not in the least," was the reply. "To attain spiritual enlightenment and become a person of serene inner life, you must take one of the texts of the Holy Scripture and meditate upon it for a long time with all your power of concentration and attention. Then the light of true knowledge will be revealed to you. The same thing may be said about the prayer. If you wish it to be pure, right and sweet take up one of the short prayers of few but strong words, and repeat it often and for a long time. Then you will savor prayer."

This instruction of the priest pleased me greatly. How practical and simple it was, and yet so profound and wise! I thanked God in my mind for showing me so good a pastor of His Church.

When we finished our meal, the priest said: "Take a rest after dinner while I read my Bible and prepare my sermon for tomorrow." I therefore made my way to the kitchen. There was no one there except a very old woman who crouched in the corner, coughing. I sat down at a small window and took the *Philocalia* out of my knapsack. As I was reading it quietly to myself, I heard the old woman in the corner incessantly whispering the Jesus Prayer. Rejoicing at the most holy Name of our Lord spoken so often, I told her: "What a good thing you do, mother, by saying the prayer constantly. It is a most Christian and most salutary one!" "Oh, yes!" she answered. "This is the only joy I have left in my life. 'Lord, have mercy on me.'"

"Have you been in the habit of saying this prayer for very long?"

"Ever since my early youth! How could I live without it, for the Prayer of Jesus saved me from destruction and death."

"How is that? Pray, tell me about it for the glory of God and the blessed power of the Jesus Prayer." I put the *Philocalia* into my knapsack and came closer, ready to listen to her story. She told me thus:

"I was a pretty girl when I was young. My parents were about to give me away in marriage, and on the eve of the wedding my bridegroom came to see us. Suddenly, when he was about a dozen paces from our house, he collapsed and died without regaining his breath. This terrified me so that I refused to marry and made up my mind to live in virginity and prayer. Though I longed for pilgrimages to holy places, I dared not go all by myself, for I was quite young and feared that wicked people might harm me. Then, an old woman pilgrim I knew taught me to recite incessantly the Prayer of Jesus in all my wanderings. If I did so, she assured me, no misfortune could ever befall me on my journey. I trusted her and, sure enough, I walked even to far-off shrines many times, and never came to grief. My parents gave me money for my travels. As I grew old and my health failed me, the priest here out of the kindness of the heart, provided me with board and lodging."

I listened to her with joy and did not know how to thank God for this day in which I had learned so much by these edifying examples of the spiritual life. Then, asking the kindly priest for his blessing, I started off on my way in gladness . . .

Having finished these tales, I said to my spiritual father: "Forgive me in God's name; I have already talked too much, and the Holy Fathers call even spiritual talk idle chatter if it is prolonged. It is time for me to meet my fellow-traveler to Jerusalem. Pray for me, a wretched sinner, that God in His mercy may prosper me on my Journey."

"With all my soul I wish it, my beloved brother in the Lord," he answered. "May the all-loving grace of God overshadow your way and guide you as the Angel Raphael guided Tobias."

ENDNOTES

1. Saint Demetrius, Metropolitan of Rostov (1651–1709) was a well-known religious writer, who composed a classical collection of the Lives of Saints in twelve volumes and a tract on the refutation of the Old Believers. He was the representative of the Kievan (i.e., the Latin scholastic) school in the Russia of Peter I.
2. These are Byzantine mystical theologians of the fourteenth century. The first Slavonic translation of the *Philocalia,* by Païsius Velichkovsky, contained the works of about thirty Greek fathers.
3. Saint Innocent, a missionary and the first Bishop of Irkutsk (1680–1731), canonized in 1805.
4. Callistus, confused in the *Philocalia* with a Patriarch of Constantinople, is probably an ascetic contemporary with the Patriarch (fourteenth century).
5. In these reasonings of the schoolmaster one sees the blending of the Orthodox doctrine on the holiness of